Smell the Coffee

A wake-up call for the Conservative Party

A study of public opinion and the Conservative Party's campaign for the 2005 general election

Michael A. Ashcroft

First published in Great Britain 2005

A catalogue record for this book is available from the British Library.

ISBN 1 904734 10 3

Printed and bound in Great Britain by CGI Europe

Published by Michael A. Ashcroft

Contents

Acknowledgements

In the introduction and the few words of conclusion to this study I have not pulled any punches. The opinions I have expressed about the challenges that face the Conservative Party are mine alone.

I hope that these comments, and the evidence I have offered to support them, will be of value to the party as it debates why we have not made progress and what we need to do to reconnect with what was once the bedrock of Conservative support: middle class voters, women, professionals and the other groups that were once part of our core vote.

The chapters describing the research programme and its conclusions speak for themselves and need no commentary from me, and it is for readers to draw their own conclusions. Those who are dubious about my interpretation of the research (or even sceptical that the results can have been as I describe) can check for themselves: the full data tables from every poll I commissioned can be found on the internet at **www.lordashcroft.com**.

It goes without saying that a report of this depth and a research programme of this scale has been an enormous undertaking. The expert pollsters from Populus and YouGov have been extraordinarily professional and great fun to work with, and my own political advisers have offered me excellent guidance. I have also received advice and suggestions from a number of prominent MPs and other figures, of various leanings, within the Conservative Party. I would like to thank them all. This study is a product of some of the best brains in the business and whether or not readers agree with the conclusion I hope they will appreciate a good job well done.

I have also drawn on a range of published polling from ICM, MORI, Communicate Research and NOP and sometimes quoted from their experts' published commentaries. While I have done this without reference to them I would like to acknowledge the value of their excellent websites.

Introduction

The Answers Are Out There

I have occasionally been a passive investor in businesses, but not so occasionally that I am unable to say with certainty that it is not for me. I much prefer to be involved - to make sure that my investment is wisely placed and, where I can, to help. Similar rules apply in respect to the charities to which I give. I like to be involved.

My financial contributions to the Conservative Party could be classified similarly, especially in recent years. What began as admiration at a distance for the work of Margaret Thatcher has grown over a twenty-year relationship with the party to a much closer association. During William Hague's time as leader, I was Treasurer of the party, and I have recently rejoined the Board. I have learned a great deal and believe I can contribute more effectively.

I am known to be a donor to the party, and I am proud of that fact. But I would not wish anyone to imagine that my financial support comes, de facto, with strings attached. There is a very clear distinction to be drawn between the exercise which I am about to introduce - which is unashamedly a contribution to the debate as to the future complexion and presentation of the party - and affluence seeking influence. In my case at least, the latter could not be further from the truth.

It was eighteen months before the 2005 general election that I decided to help the Conservative Party's campaign in target seats. I was impressed by the discipline that Michael Howard bought to the party as its new leader and having taken a relatively low profile because of business commitments in recent years I decided to get more involved again.

I am conscious in electing to publish this report now, that I do so during the preliminary skirmishes of a contest to decide the future leader of the party. I have little doubt that, before the ink on this document is even dry, more than one of the contenders will seize upon these findings as proof positive that only they are capable of delivery against these findings.

I should make it clear that this report is a contribution to the debate about what the party does now to reconnect with the lost voters who will form a part of a winning coalition in the future. In this pamphlet, I have not set out to criticise personally those responsible for the General Election campaign.

Like the time it takes to change the course of a super tanker, the appointment of Lynton Crosby was too late to make a significant difference. Michael Howard fought a determined campaign and restored discipline to the party. The campaign was professional and vigorous. We need to look back at the campaign and learn the lessons of our devastating defeat but then we must look forward and renew our party so that it wins again.

I welcome the fact that there will be discussion - even disagreement - about this work. Indeed, I would be disappointed if it were otherwise. I would, though, make just one request. And I will answer just one question before it is even asked.

My request is that those who wish to comment on these findings do so only after reading them, and after giving them due consideration. A great deal of thought and effort from some very talented and diligent people went into completing this exercise. They deserve equal thoughtfulness from those who wish to assess this work.

My answer to the question that has yet to be asked is, No. I have not produced this document in order to support any one candidate for the leadership. I hope all of them will read it and learn from it. I wish all of them well as we embark upon what will undoubtedly prove to be a testing as well as vital time for the party.

The work on this publication, in fact started back in the middle of 2004 when it was clear that the candidates to whose local efforts I had contributed were not making the headway that their labours warranted. Though under no illusions about the scale of the task that faced the Conservatives at the election I was puzzled that many of these exceptional candidates, running energetic and positive campaigns focused on issues that mattered most to their prospective constituents, were not reporting a better response.

My puzzlement only increased when the Conservative co-chairman, Lord Saatchi, reported in the autumn of 2004 that the party had concluded from its private research that it was in fact heading for victory in 103 of the 130 most marginal Labour seats. This was a much-needed boost to morale among staff and volunteers, but I feared that this conclusion was seriously flawed and that the decision to target more than 164 constituencies (which included 34 Lib Dem held seats), many of which barely qualified as marginals, may have been a serious mistake.

Successive dismal and entirely expected general election defeats had not muted the Conservatives' insistence that published opinion polls were not to be trusted. But it seemed to me that despite the politician's mantra that the result of the General Election was "the only poll that matters", it was usually depressingly similar to that forecast by all the other polls in the preceding weeks and months. The published polls had not been seriously wrong about a general election result since 1992, and the habit of dismissing their findings now appeared less to do with healthy scepticism or cheerful optimism than a turning away from reality. Although the party carried out its own research, the conclusions were at odds with all the other available evidence, the strength of which the party failed to see. The belief that the party was on the verge of winning an election seemed implausible, blinkered and naïve.

I therefore decided to commission my own programme of research, with the aim of establishing the real state of public opinion on the questions that would determine the outcome of the general election: not only the true level of support for the parties but the underlying attributes associated with each. I wanted to find out whether the picture in marginal seats really was different from that in Britain as a whole, and whether the 164-seat battleground made sense; whether Conservative fortunes could be turned around through policies and issues or whether the party's problem was deeper; and why it was that many of the candidates I had decided to help fund were finding it so difficult to build support.

Over the course of seven months I commissioned twelve pieces of research: five surveys of the battleground on which the party would take on Labour; an examination of the situation in seats the party was defending against the Liberal Democrats; a series of polls in individual marginal constituencies; a batch of focus groups in key seats; a tracking poll that monitored daily movements in opinion from January to the election; post-election surveys in the battleground and across the country; and what was, to the best of my knowledge, the biggest national political poll ever conducted in Britain.

It was clear to me that after the election the party was going to have to face up to some hard facts and I decided at the time I commissioned this polling that following the election I would publish my findings as a contribution to that debate. I have been a life-long Conservative and I passionately believe that Britain deserves a Conservative Party that is once again fit to govern and champion our values of freedom, enterprise and opportunity. I hope this report will contribute to the debate about working out how to get back on that track.

This research established that the Conservatives were doing no better nationally than they had in 2001. But crucially, on the battleground of marginal seats, they were doing little better than they were nationally; certainly there was no evidence that the party was poised for victory across vast tracts of marginal Labour territory. From the outset, the party's list of 164 target seats looked woefully long and threatened to limit rather than maximise the number of Conservative gains at the election.

We learned that while other parties' supporters had a similar profile to Britain as a whole, Conservatives did not. Not surprisingly, their attitudes to contemporary social and cultural issues were often different to those of other people, and their view of the Conservative Party's prospects was wildly divergent from that of the swing voters whose support the Conservatives needed to attract.

Though none of the parties inspired the devoted admiration of the public, the Conservatives were thought less likely than their opponents to care about ordinary people's problems, share the values of voters or deliver what they promised. Majorities in key marginal seats thought the party was out of touch, had failed to learn from its mistakes, cared more about the well-off than have-nots, and did not stand for opportunity for all. And things did not improve with time - voters had a more negative view of the Conservative Party at the end of the campaign than they did at the beginning.

The issue that dominated the Conservative campaign, immigration, was never important enough to voters to determine how large numbers of them would cast their votes, however strongly they agreed with the Tory position. Those who thought the Conservatives had the best policy on immigration but trusted Labour more on the economy, supported Labour by a huge margin.

To the extent that the party had identified concerns that people shared, it had failed to articulate solutions, and on the issues that mattered most to people, Labour's lead remained unassailable - or at least, unassailed. People did not feel the Conservatives shared their aspirations or their priorities, and for two thirds of voters the answer to the ubiquitous question "are you thinking what we're thinking?" was "No". Conservative support among the AB social group - the professionals and managers among whom the party has always achieved large majorities when it is winning elections - fell even from the historically low level achieved at the general election of 2001.

It was clear throughout that Tony Blair had lost the trust of a large proportion of voters, but that a sizeable majority would still prefer him as prime minister to Michael Howard. Gordon Brown, meanwhile, was much more popular than either. Combined with voters' conviction that the Labour Party had changed forever, this rendered previously mooted Tory warnings of a Brown premiership in the event of a Labour victory harmless or even counterproductive. (The idea that Britain would fear a socialist revolution in the event of Mr Brown entering Number 10 was regarded as merely fanciful).

For pollsters, elections are the acid test. Our research proved depressingly accurate, forecasting almost the exact swing from Labour to the Conservatives in the battleground seats and coming within a percentage point of predicting the level of party support nationally. In fact, at this election all the final published polls were within a few percentage points of the result. The refrain that the polls are not reliable and don't detect what is happening on the ground will no longer wash. Of course individual polls will be wrong from time to time. But overall, the polls were right. They can be believed. And they are worth listening to, not just because they have said clearly, for years, that the Conservatives were not close to power, but because they have explained why.

The Conservative Party's problem is its brand. Conservatives loathe being told this but it is an inescapable fact. Tony Blair once said that he knew the 1992 election was lost when he met a man washing his car. The man said he had always voted Labour in the past, but now that he had started his own business he was going to vote Tory. The Conservative Party, in other words, was associated not just with success but with aspiration, with getting on in life. What is it associated with now? Not with those things, or opportunity for all, or economic competence, or the delivery of good public services, or with looking after the less fortunate, or with life in modern Britain.

To the extent that the voters who rejected us in 2005 associate the Conservative Party with anything at all it is with the past, with policies for the privileged few and with lack of leadership. We cannot hope to win a general election while this is how we are seen by people who should be our supporters.

Many in the party are already turning their minds as to how we can rebuild our support, and the interesting policy agendas that are emerging are to be welcomed. But we must realise that interesting policy agendas are not in themselves sufficient. The brand problem means that the most robust, coherent, principled and attractive Conservative policies will have no impact on the voters who mistrust our motivation and doubt our ability to deliver.

After previous defeats too many Conservatives have been too ready to learn only the lessons that suited them. After the Labour landslide of 1997, for example, a theory did the rounds that not only had a million Tory voters switched to the Referendum Party or UKIP, but millions more had stayed at home. This was not, as it happened, true (over 2 million 1992 Tories switched directly to Labour), but that did not discourage some commentators from declaring that the answer for the Conservative Party was simply to mobilise the heartland.

No such nonsense has yet emerged in the aftermath of May 2005. Yet the temptation is always to make the most of crumbs of comfort. Perhaps one cannot blame Michael Howard for his declaration on 6 May that the Conservative performance at the election represented a huge step forward, but it didn't. Our share of the vote rose by just half of one per cent, and in the Labour-held seats which, by definition, the Conservative Party must win if it is ever to form a government again, our vote share fell. Our candidates ran some exceptional campaigns but there is no hiding from the fact that many of our gains occurred because Labour voters switched to the Liberal Democrats and not because we succeeded in attracting new votes for the Conservatives. We can only win a general election if we can get large numbers of Labour voters to switch to us.

There are many lessons to be learned from the 2005 election, and I hope that the evidence in this study will help us to grasp them.

- We must target our resources more effectively.
- We must campaign hardest on the things that matter most to people, rather than things we hope can be made to matter.
- With a number of other parties competing for votes we must never assume that Labour's unpopularity will translate directly into support for the Conservatives.
- We must realise that appealing to the conservative or even reactionary instincts of people who in reality are never going to support the Conservatives in large numbers prevents us from connecting with our real core vote and means we will never attract the support of minority communities that we should seek to serve too.
- We must recreate that real core vote - the election-winning coalition of professionals, women, and aspirational voters without whom the party risks becoming a rump.

More than anything else we must make sure we understand Britain as it is today, and how Britain sees us. Until we do we will just continue talking to ourselves.

Chapter One

Drawing the Battleground (or 'To Defend Everything is to Defend Nothing')

"School discipline. More police. Cleaner hospitals. Lower taxes. Controlled immigration".

Seven months to the day before the general election of 5 May 2005, at the Conservative Party Conference in Bournemouth, Michael Howard unveiled the ten words that would constitute the basis of his campaign.

The autumn party conferences are always of more interest to political journalists and activists than to the voters whose attention they seek, but the 2004 season was unusually noteworthy. As well as being the last opportunity each party would have to dominate the news before the expected election, it offered a platform from which Labour or the Conservatives might open up a sustained lead after a long period in which polls had suggested they were neck and neck.

The average of all published polls had for ten months put the two parties within two points of each other. In October 2004, though, average Labour support was recorded at 37%, 6 points ahead of the Tories.

A YouGov poll for the Daily Telegraph[1] published during the conference had found that only 19% of voters felt the Conservatives were "ready for power and look like a government in waiting". Only just over a quarter (26%) thought Michael Howard was providing strong leadership, and barely a third agreed that the Conservatives "know how to run a successful low tax economy" or that "the Conservatives nowadays are sensible and moderate" (34% each). More than two thirds (68%) agreed that "it was hard to know what the Conservatives stand for at the moment" (68%), and exactly half of voters thought the party was "irrelevant – they just seem out of it".

---

1 Conducted 27-29 September 2004, published in the Daily Telegraph 4 October 2004.

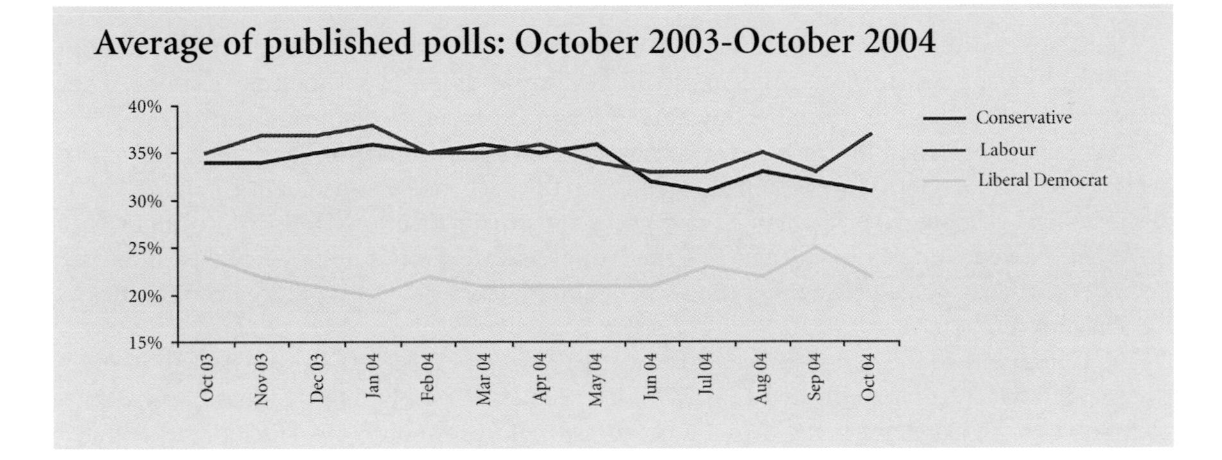

A further poll looking in detail at people's attitudes to the three main parties[2] had brought further bad news for the Conservatives. Less than a third of voters thought the party had a good team of leaders, shared their values, was honest and principled, or understood the way people lived their lives in today's Britain. Crucially, more than half of the 75% of voters saying they were dissatisfied with the Labour government said they would still prefer it to the Conservatives, and only half of the 68% who thought Tony Blair had not been a good prime minister overall would rather have had Michael Howard in Downing Street.

The poll also found that 53% of voters agreed with the proposition that "the Conservative Party doesn't seem to stand for anything anymore", and a 70% thought "the Conservatives just attack the government over whatever happens to be in the news, but never say anything positive". Only 38% thought the party "would do a good job of running the country", the same proportion that said it had "changed for the better since it was kicked out in 1997".

For Conservatives inclined to dismiss opinion polls, the Hartlepool by-election on 30 September, brought about by Peter Mandelson's appointment as a European Commissioner, had been a salutary event. From second place in the constituency at the 2001 general election the Conservatives dropped to fourth, winning only 9.7% of the vote - behind not only Labour and the Liberal Democrats, but the United Kingdom Independence Party.

Just months from a general election, then, the Conservative Party appeared to have made no progress – or even to have fallen back - since Tony Blair's second landslide victory of 7 June 2001, in which Labour were returned to office with 42% of the vote in Great Britain to the Tories' 33%.

2 Conducted by Populus between 2-5 September 2004 and published in The Times throughout the conference season.

The Conservatives saw things differently. They argued that not only was the Hartlepool result irrelevant, the apparently bleak national picture was misleading since it took no account of the marginal constituencies in which the outcome of the next general election would be decided.

After being appointed the party's co-chairman by Michael Howard in November 2003, Lord Saatchi had discovered that under Iain Duncan Smith the party had planned to target only 94 seats at the general election, 70 fewer than it would need for a majority in the House of Commons.

"When I asked why it is not a list of 164, the answer was we did not think we could win them," he said. "Michael is absolutely not interested in the situation where we just reduce Labour's majority. The aim is to win".[3]

The Conservatives duly set their sights on a battleground of at least 164 seats (though in practice the party's target list numbered 180). Within a year, Lord Saatchi reported that in these seats the party was not just doing better than it was nationally, it was winning. On 4 October he revealed to the Conservative National Convention the conclusions drawn from private research by the party's pollster, Opinion Research Business, in 130 marginal constituencies held by Labour and a further 34 held by the Liberal Democrats. Of the 130 Labour marginals, the Conservatives were on course to win 103, with Labour's share of the vote falling from 47% in 2001 to 35%, and the Tories up from 36% to 39% - a swing of 7.5%.[4] "The explanation is that the national polls are an average of everything", he said. "These target seats are seats in which by definition there is a higher propensity to vote Conservative".[5]

The reliability of these conclusions was questioned in other quarters, for three reasons. First, the party did not give details of the polls' timing and sample sizes, or the precise questions asked. As Nick Sparrow, director of ICM Research, commented: "If an organisation doing a private poll is not prepared to release information to allow people to make up their own minds about the validity of the research, you should treat it with caution".[6]

Secondly, when set against the national picture the claim of a Conservative lead across the battleground seats looked incongruous. The five polls conducted in the weeks before the co-chairman revealed his analysis produced results ranging from a 7-point Labour lead to a 1-point Tory lead[7] – a picture that inevitably cast doubt on the suggestion that the Conservatives were already on course to take back over 100 marginal constituencies, many of which would require a significant swing.

---

3 Sunday Times, 7 March 2004.

4 Financial Times, 6 October 2004.

5 Birmingham Post, 5 October 2004

6 Financial Times, 6 October 2004

7 Populus 30 September-2 October; ICM/Guardian 17-19 September; MORI 10-14 September; YouGov/Telegraph 21-23 September; Communicate/Independent on Sunday 27-28 September.

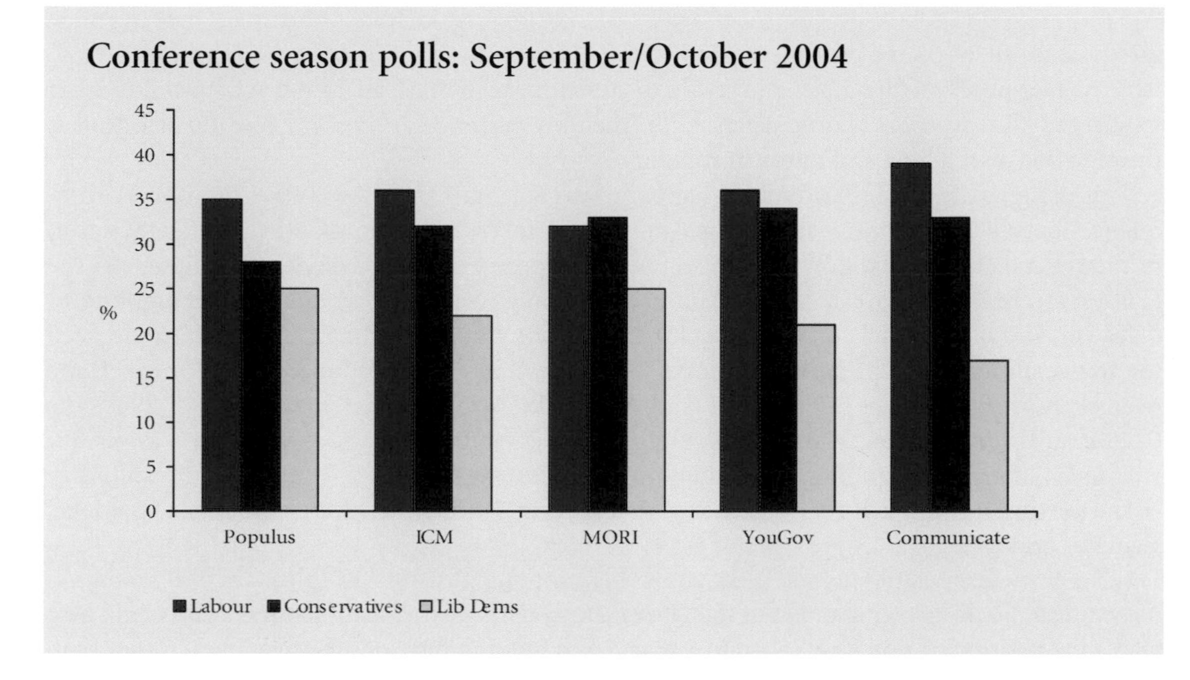

Thirdly, what published evidence there was from marginal constituencies was not altogether consistent with the party's reported private polling. In June 2004 ICM conducted a poll in a combination of 202 Labour-Conservative, Labour-Liberal Democrat and Conservative-Liberal Democrat marginals[8]. Although the survey was based on a rather different selection of constituencies than those on which the party based its claim, it was nevertheless the best publicly available research on marginal seats at the time and gave a picture of the state of the parties in the places that would decide the outcome of the general election.

ICM found the Conservatives on 33% across these 202 seats, 5 points ahead of Labour – a swing of 3.5% to the Conservatives. If typical, such a swing would mean Labour losing the seats in which they had a majority of 7% or less over the Conservatives, of which there were 24 – far from the 103 in which the Tories claimed to be set for victory.

But whatever doubts others might have had about the co-chairman's confidence in the Conservatives' private polling data, the episode was significant. Not only did it give the Tory faithful in Bournemouth some hope (as one senior Tory remarked, "I believe everything Lord Saatchi

8 Conducted 1-3 June 2004; published in the News of the World 6 June 2004.

says because it cheers me up"[9]), it confirmed the Conservative strategy. The party would fight to win 164 marginal constituencies and return to government in one leap. Moreover, it would expect to succeed. "In my view," Lord Saatchi said, "the only way we can possibly lose this election is through our own failing and our own stupidity".[10]

This designation of the electoral battleground was a gamble that would have profound consequences both for the Conservative campaign over the following seven months and for the result of the general election itself. By focusing on a smaller group of more winnable constituencies the Conservatives might have a better chance of winning seats, but would risk accusations of defeatism and playing only for a respectable second place. But in targeting every seat it would need for an overall majority, the party's resources would inevitably be spread more thinly. In its efforts to reclaim seats such as Tynemouth and Wakefield, with Labour majorities of 20%, the Conservatives might make it more difficult for themselves to win seats where a much lower but still ambitious swing (and huge campaigning resources) were needed. More seriously still, they risked leaving undefended marginal Conservative seats, 19 of which were vulnerable to a local swing of only 3%.

For a party in a position to take great strides back into territory lost to Labour in 1997 and hold its own against the growing threat of the Liberal Democrats, the 164-seat battleground could be a viable proposition. If not, it was a strategy that risked holding the Conservatives back, rather than smoothing progress on their path to power. The party had decided on the basis of its private research that it was up to the job.

There was little other evidence available to support their conclusion. The first of a series of polls I commissioned in the battleground seats[11] found that in the autumn of 2004 the situation in these constituencies was very similar to that in the country as a whole.

A Populus poll for the Times[12] conducted at the same time as this research gave Labour a 34% to 33% lead nationally, and a YouGov poll for the Telegraph[13] two weeks later put Labour ahead by 35% to 32% across the country. And in the 164 battleground seats, where the Conservatives claimed to be ahead, our research found them trailing by a similar margin, on 33% to Labour's 35%.

In the 130 most marginal Labour seats where the Conservatives were second, Labour were ahead 36%-33% (the same size gap that YouGov's November poll found for Britain as a whole).

9 Financial Times, 6 October 2004

10 Birmingham Post, 5 October 2004. The remark echoed his claim at the party's Spring Forum, following research suggesting the Conservatives had a small lead on tax and the economy, that "it is now possible not only to see how we will win the next election but it is hard to see how we will lose". (Independent, 13 March 2004)

11 Poll A: see Appendix 1.

12 Conducted 5-7 November 2004, published in The Times 9-10 November 2004.

13 Conducted 23-25 November 2004, published in the Daily Telegraph 26 November, sample 2,044.

While this represented a considerable narrowing of the margin since 2001, when Labour had won these seats by 48%-36%, the Conservative share of the vote had actually fallen, and the swing from Labour to the Conservatives was only 4.5%. This was enough to win back seats with a Labour majority over the Conservatives of 9% or less, of which there were 38: far from the 103 that were supposedly leaning their way. Nearly half (49%) of voters in these 130 seats expected Labour to win in their constituency, compared to 26% who anticipated having a Conservative MP after the election.

The Tories were 5 points ahead in the 34 most marginal seats in which they had come second to the Liberal Democrats in 2001, with Labour and the Liberal Democrats each on 29%. If replicated at the general election the swing of 7% would have been enough to topple a further 23 seats. Even so, as in the Labour territory only just over a quarter (26%) of voters here expected the Conservatives to win their seat, while 59% expected the Liberal Democrats to hold on.

Across the whole battleground, voters preferred a Labour government led by Tony Blair to a Conservative government led by Michael Howard by 54% to 46%. While this gap narrowed to 6 points in the Labour marginals, in Liberal Democrat territory, where the Conservatives were ahead, voters preferred Tony Blair and Labour by 58% to 42%.

More voters in the battleground seats thought Labour were doing very or fairly badly at governing the country (55%) than thought they were doing very or fairly well (43%). However, Labour were thought doing much better than the Conservatives were doing at their job of providing an alternative government: 69% thought the Tories were doing badly on this score, while less than a quarter (24%) thought they were doing well. Battleground voters thought the Liberal Democrats were performing better in the alternative government stakes: 41% thought they were doing well with only 45% saying the opposite, the lowest negative rating of the three.

A separate poll[14] confirmed the picture. This survey was intended to replicate as far as possible the methodology assumed to have been used in the Conservatives' private research – telephone interviews in the 130 seats where ORB had conducted its research for the party, 103 of which it said it was set to win. This second poll put the Conservatives on 32% in the 130 Labour seats, 6 points behind Labour – a swing of 3% since 2001, enough to win back only 22 Labour seats.

In the 34 most marginal Liberal Democrat seats, in contrast to the first battleground poll, the Conservatives trailed the incumbents by 5 points, 39% to 34%. This represented only a 2% swing to the Tories, enough to capture only 10 of their target Liberal Democrat seats.

The research found that at this stage voters recalled low rates of contact with political parties. By the beginning of November only 6% of people in Labour marginals and 5% in Liberal Democrat mar-

14 Poll B: see Appendix 1.

ginals had been visited by the Conservatives, fewer than by their principal opponents. While Conservative leaflets had reached 23% of voters in Labour-held targets and 29% in Liberal Democrat marginals, this compared to the 37% and 44% who had received Labour and Liberal Democrat literature in the same places. The Conservatives were also behind on sending personally addressed letters (10% v 12% against Labour; 9% v 14% against the Liberal Democrats) and distributing questionnaires (6% v 9% against Labour; 6% v 13% against the Liberal Democrats).

Conservative candidates also appeared to have made a less positive impression than the MPs they were challenging on the constituents they aspired to represent. In both Labour and Liberal Democrat seats, sitting Members were thought more likely than their Conservative opponents to live in the constituency, to be closely involved locally, to do a good job on key local issues, to work hard for people with problems, and to contact voters between elections. While these findings illustrate the power of incumbency, it may also be the case that this power has increased since MPs were given substantially increased allowances to help them communicate with their electors.

The findings suggested that the Conservatives were perhaps not following with sufficient vigour the dictum of their ally John Howard, prime minister of Australia and former employer of their newly-appointed campaign director, Lynton Crosby, that "you can't fatten the pig on market day".

A few weeks later I commissioned polls in nine constituencies where the Liberal Democrats were a close second to the Conservatives[15]. Five of these were held by members of the shadow cabinet whom the Liberal Democrats hoped to dislodge as part of their so-called "decapitation" strategy of targeting senior Conservatives. The poll suggested that in these seats the Conservatives had actually lost ground since 2001, with voters swinging to the Liberal Democrats.

To take account of the likelihood that during the campaign the parties would tell voters, if they did not already know, that they lived in a marginal constituency, the poll reminded supporters of parties other than the Conservatives and Liberal Democrats that the election in their seat would be a close race between the two and asked whether this would make any difference to their voting intention. In the "decapitation" seats, these voters were told that the Liberal Democrats were trying to defeat a named Conservative MP. These reminders produced an even greater swing, as Labour voters in particular switched to the party in the best position to beat the Tories.

However, there were differences in behaviour between the two types of seat. In "non-decapitation" seats, where other parties' voters were simply told that their constituency was a two-horse race between the Conservatives and Liberal Democrats, 40% said they would vote for their first choice regardless, with nearly a quarter (23%) unsure what they would do.

15 Folkestone & Hythe, Orpington, Taunton, Eastbourne, Surrey South West, Dorset West, Maidenhead, Haltemprice & Howden and Westmoreland & Lonsdale. Poll C: see Appendix 1.

In the "decapitation" seats, voters for parties other than the Conservatives and Liberal Democrats were told "the Liberal Democrats have said they will campaign especially hard in your seat because the Conservative MP, [named], who is a senior figure in the party and expected to be a Cabinet minister if the Tories were to win the general election. The Liberal Democrats think they could do real damage to the future prospects of the Conservative Party by winning in your constituency". The other parties' voters were much less willing to be complicit in such a scheme than they were simply to vote tactically in an ordinary two-horse race. While the numbers saying they would switch to the Liberal Democrats or the Conservatives remained steady, the proportions saying they would vote for their first-choice party rose by half, to 60%, with "don't knows" falling to just 6%. It was clear that if voters understood what the Liberal Democrats were asking them to do, the "decapitation strategy" was less likely to work.

Facing a swing against them of 1.9% in the "non-decapitation" seats and 3.9% in the "decapitation" seats, at the beginning of December 2004 the Conservatives looked set for very tight contests in Taunton, Orpington, South West Surrey, Dorset West, Haltemprice & Howden, Westmoreland & Lonsdale and Maidenhead (presenting a threat to the Shadow Chancellor, Oliver Letwin, the Shadow Home Secretary, David Davis, and the Shadow Education Secretary, Tim Collins).

The 130-seat Labour-Conservative battleground: autumn 2004

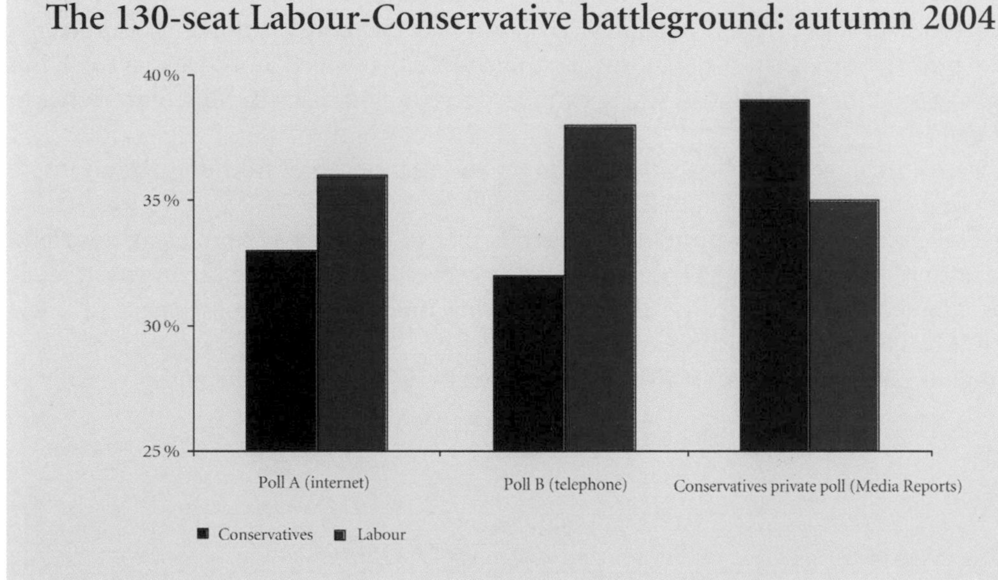

Polls A and B (see appendix 1), Conservative Party/Opinion Research Business (Media Reports)

It is worth noting that most voters in marginal seats did not realise at this stage that they lived on the battleground. Our autumn research found that only 38% of voters correctly identified the constituency in which they lived as being a marginal, while 36% thought it was safe with a big majority for the incumbent. More than a quarter (26%) didn't know which category it fell into.

So by Christmas 2004, the available evidence suggested that by targeting 164 constituencies for outright victory, the Conservatives risked making a strategic error. Independent research had suggested that on current form they would gain fewer than 40 of their target Labour seats. Though the picture on Liberal Democrat territory was ambiguous, even with the most optimistic interpretation of the research the potential gains were not enough to mount a serious challenge to Labour's Commons majority, and there was even evidence that the Tories risked losing MPs of their own.

The most marginal seats where the Conservatives had the best chance of victory would by definition be very close races. Labour and the Liberal Democrats would heavily defend their vulnerable territory, and no seats would fall without a fierce battle. All in all, there was already good reason to fear that seats towards the bottom of the list of 164 would prove beyond the reach of the Conservatives in 2005, and that the finite campaigning resources the party had at its disposal would therefore be better directed at, say, the or so 50 seats in which they had the most credible prospect of victory.

Otherwise, they faced the prospect of failing to win not only the more ambitious constituencies (in some of which they needed a swing more than three times that which looked achievable), but tightly-fought seats at the top of the list where extra resources might make the difference between victory and defeat.

In other words, by targeting 50 seats the Conservatives might emerge from the election with more MPs than if they targeted 164.

To adapt Frederick the Great, who told his generals that to defend everything was to defend nothing, by setting their sights on 164 seats the Conservatives effectively had no targets at all. A strategy was adopted that depended on the party making more progress in the space of a few months than it had achieved in the previous ten years.

The last poll of 2004 put Labour on 40%, with the Conservatives 9 points behind.[16]

16 ICM in the Guardian, conducted on 16-19 December 2004, published 21 December 2004.

Chapter Two

The Phoney War

Early January has long been regarded as the best moment to take a reading of the levels of support for each party. With little political news or activity over the Christmas break people tend to tune out of politics and current affairs, providing an ideal opportunity to gauge voters' views with minimal adulteration from passing news events.

The consistency of the Conservatives' January poll findings – which inspired the term 'flatlining', now part of the political lexicon - are therefore a compelling illustration of the party's performance. They demonstrate a failure to win back support not just since the 2001 general election, or since they lost power in 1997, but since the public lost confidence in John Major's government in the early 1990s.

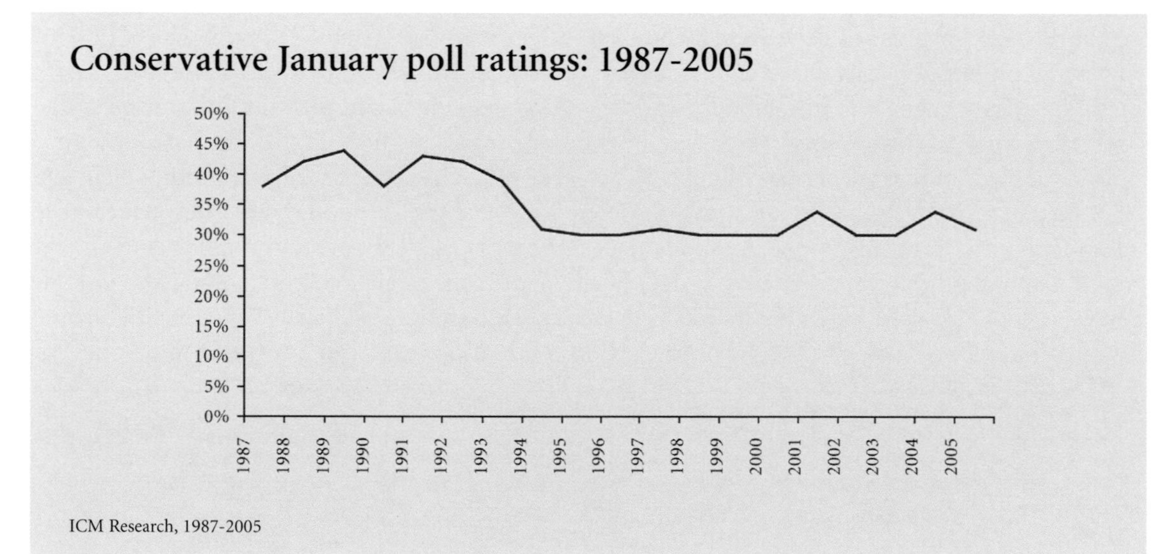

Conservative January poll ratings: 1987-2005

ICM Research, 1987-2005

In January 1993, four months after Britain's departure from the Exchange Rate Mechanism, ICM recorded Conservative support at 39%. The government fell in popularity throughout that year, particularly in the wake of the tax-raising budget that included the imposition of VAT on fuel. By January 1994 the Tories were at 31% where they remained, within the margin of error, every January for eleven years.

ICM's January poll rating had also been a reliable guide to Conservative performance in the two general elections held during this period. In January 1997 they put the Tories on 31%, exactly the share of the vote the party received in Labour's first landslide. In January 2001 they polled at 34%, 1 point better than they did in Labour's second[17].

Peter Kellner, chairman of YouGov, commented on the 2005 New Year polls: "The figures for the Conservatives are grim. Apart from two short-lived spurts in support – the petrol crisis in September 2000 and the first few months of Michael Howard's leadership – the Tories have been flatlining at 30%-33% for the past 12 years. A small consolation is that they could gain seats even if their vote share slips back slightly. They seem likely, though, to end up for the third successive election with well under 200 MPs, a fate they suffered only once between 1835 and 1992".[18]

'The Polls are Wrong' and Other Fallacies

The Conservatives claimed that such a gloomy interpretation of their prospects was mistaken. The party prepared a dossier for Conservative MPs on 4 February entitled 'Overstating Labour', which argued that polls had consistently overestimated Labour support in every election since 1995 and implied that they would do so again.

The dossier's analysis was flawed and incomplete. After the 1992 general election (in which "not one single poll produced results that even hinted that John Major would win by a margin of 8%")[19] ICM made significant changes to its methods to address the systematic bias against the Conservatives that resulted in what the dossier emphasised was "probably the biggest polling failure there has ever been".[20]

By adopting random telephone polling ICM achieved much more representative samples than had been possible with face-to-face interviewing. Voters for one party or another are often reluctant to admit their view, or to answer poll questions at all, if the party they support is unpopular, and an otherwise demographically representative sample can therefore start off with too many supporters of one party. So ICM also used weighting measures to ensure samples were politically representative, based on how interviewees voted at the previous election. They also introduced a formula to account for

17 Polls conducted 3-5 January 1997, sample 1,201, and 19-21 January 2001, sample 1,004.

18 Sunday Times, 6 February 2005. Party strategists used the term "flatlining" to describe the Conservative performance in presentations to the shadow cabinet as early as September 1998. It appeared in the media in this context as early as 2000 (Daily Telegraph, 5 May; Guardian 11 May) and was adopted by other eminent pollsters such as Sir Robert Worcester (eg. The Times, 4 January 2003)

19 'Overstating Labour: How polling since 1955 has overestimated Labour support', February 2005.

20 Ibid.

voters who said they didn't know how they would vote when in fact they just didn't want to say.

As a result of these changes, ICM's polls became much more accurate than those of companies which did not respond to the problems of 1992 (and who therefore continued to replicate the systematic bias in subsequent elections). But the dossier overlooked this key point. It frequently quoted figures from companies that still used the old methods, or used composite figures ("the average overstate for Labour during the whole election of 2001 was 6%") that lumped together a pollster whose methods had proved very accurate with those that still operated as they had in 1992.

The final page of the dossier urged MPs to "remember" that "in January 2001 Labour had a lead of 19%. They won by 9% - a loss of 10%". It was quoting a poll by MORI[21], which put Labour on 50% to the Conservatives' 31%. Had the dossier taken account of the ICM poll from the same week[22], which put Labour 10 points ahead on 44% - only 1 point off their eventual margin of victory in the election – this argument would have had rather less force.

One claim in particular betrayed an alarmingly weak grasp of polling methodology. The dossier noted that a higher proportion of Conservative supporters said they would definitely turn out and vote than those of other parties, and that this differential had widened since 2001. While this was true, the subsequent claim that this represented "around 1 million" extra votes since 2001 that were, by implication, ignored in the polls was emphatically not. All political pollsters now ask respondents how likely they are to vote and, in different ways, factor these answers into their calculations of voting intention. The prospect of differential turnout did not therefore represent a hidden army of undetected Tory voters because pollsters had already taken this phenomenon into account. Had they not done so, Conservative poll ratings would have been even lower than they were.

After the 2001 election pollsters continued to apply lessons from their experiences since 1992: MORI and NOP refined their methods, reducing the likelihood of them understating Conservative support as they had in the past (indeed NOP went on to get the 2005 election result exactly right in their final campaign poll for The Independent. Furthermore some of the companies that had understated Conservative support in the past stopped polling on politics altogether - most notably Gallup - and the new pollsters that emerged - Populus and YouGov - each, in their different ways, reflected in their methodologies the changes that ICM had pioneered after 1992. So while insisting that the polls had been wrong before and would be proved wrong again, the Conservatives overlooked the fact that political polling was likely to be much more accurate in 2005 than it had ever been in the past.[23]

---

21 Conducted 18-22 January 2001, published in The Times 26 January 2001, sample 2,083.

22 Conducted 19-21 January 2001, published in the Guardian 23 January 2001, sample 1.004.

23 I attended one of the sessions at which the dossier was presented to Conservative MPs and others. Given the importance of maintaining morale, it would have been inappropriate for me to point out its flaws. My more serious concern was that the party leadership did not consider it an exercise in keeping spirits up, but that they actually believed their own argument.

But perhaps the most depressing aspect of this exercise was the fact that it happened at all. The party's instinct was to see if it could find reasons for doubting the overwhelming evidence that it was staring defeat in the face.

Whatever its authors thought, the exercise failed. No wonder one MP described the dossier as "a pretty unconvincing attempt to persuade us we are not heading for the firing squad".[24]

The Big Picture

In January 2005, to measure attitudes with the most robust degree of accuracy possible, I commissioned the biggest poll of its kind ever undertaken in Britain. The nationally representative sample of 10,000 adults was enough to provide sub-samples of more than 1,000 for each age range and region[25], allowing a meaningful analysis of the differences between different demographic groups and providing a telling profile of the support of each party compared to the profile of Britain as a whole. And as well as providing a detailed picture of the political landscape at the beginning of the election year, the exercise afforded an opportunity for a survey of social and cultural attitudes in contemporary Britain.

Politically, the poll demonstrated that although Labour had a clear lead over the Conservatives, substantial numbers of voters had yet to decide how to vote and more than three quarters of these were willing to consider at least two parties. The research went beyond voting intention to quantify underlying attitudes, showing that for most people, on most measures, none of the parties on offer came up to scratch: though mixed views were expressed on parties' competence and the extent to which each cared about ordinary people's problems, none of them was thought on balance to share the values of voters, and in any case, none of them would do what they promised if they were elected.

Socially and culturally, the research found that people were proud of Britain and considered it a better country to live than it was a generation ago. They unambiguously welcomed Britain's racial, cultural and religious diversity and felt strongly that people's private behaviour, including their family arrangements, was not a matter for politicians. In these broader questions the poll revealed differences – and sometimes gulfs – in attitude between existing Conservative voters and most of Britain.

The poll found Labour 8 points ahead of the Conservatives by 39.6% to 31.6%, with the Liberal Democrats on 20.3%. (This reflected the picture presented by most national polls conducted around the same time: NOP gave Labour a 9-point lead, ICM 7 points, MORI 6 points and Populus 5 points, but YouGov 1 point[26]). Labour led among nearly all groups: the Conservatives

24 The Guardian, 25 February 2005

25 Poll D: see Appendix 1.

26 NOP 7-9 January, published in the Independent 11 January, sample 951 -- ICM 21-23 January, Guardian 25 January, 1,000 -- MORI 20-24 January, Observer 30 January, 1,051 -- Populus 7-9 January, Times 11 January, 1,506 -- YouGov 25-25 January, Telegraph 28 January, 1,965.

were ahead only among voters aged over 55 and, by thin margins, voters in the south east and the professionals and managers who constitute social group AB.

Party support by age group: January 2005

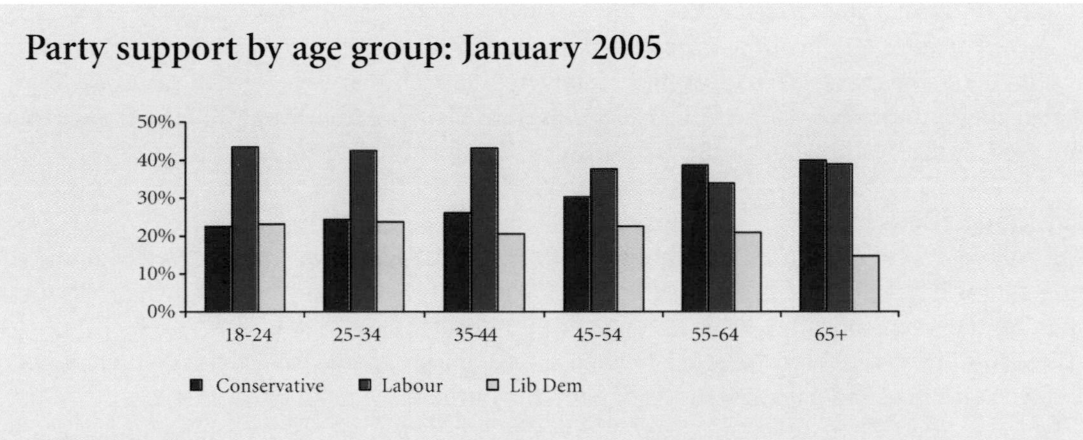

Poll D (See Appendix 1)

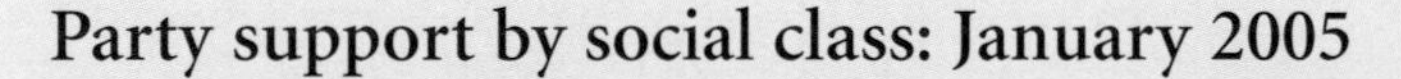

Party support by social class: January 2005

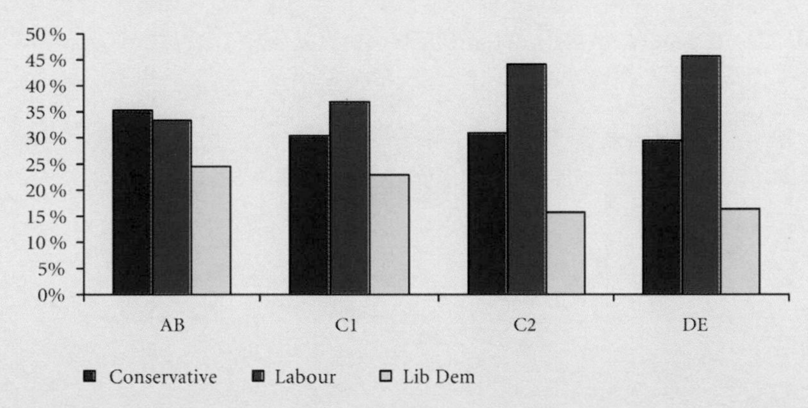

AB: senior professionals & managers (25% of the electorate); C1: junior managers/all other non-manual workers (29% of the electorate); C2: skilled manual workers (21% of the electorate); DE: semi-skilled & unskilled workers/welfare dependents (25% of the electorate)

Poll D (See Appendix 1)

However, Conservative supporters were the most certain in their support, with 82% saying they were unlikely to change their mind before the general election. Labour supporters were close behind on 79%, whereas only just over two thirds of Liberal Democrats (67%) said they were unlikely to transfer their allegiance.

Men were more certain of their voting intention, with 77% saying they were fairly sure how they would vote compared to 72% of women. Younger voters felt that they were much more likely to change their minds. Only 60% of 18-24 year olds were fairly sure they would vote as they currently intended, rising steadily though the age ranges to 86% for those aged 65 and over.

The Undecideds

The poll then went on to probe the attitudes of the nearly one in five voters (19%) who said they didn't know how they would vote, or refused to say. 46% of this group (9% of the whole electorate) said that they were a floating voter who had not yet decided how to vote.

One third of swing voters (who might change their mind) and floating voters (who had not yet decided) said they had not ruled out voting for any of the three main parties.

However, the Conservatives and Labour had equal numbers of resolute opponents: 18% said they definitely would not vote Conservative but were undecided between Labour and the Liberal Democrats, the same proportion as that which would definitely not vote Labour and were undecided between the other two parties. Only 8% said that of the three main parties they had only

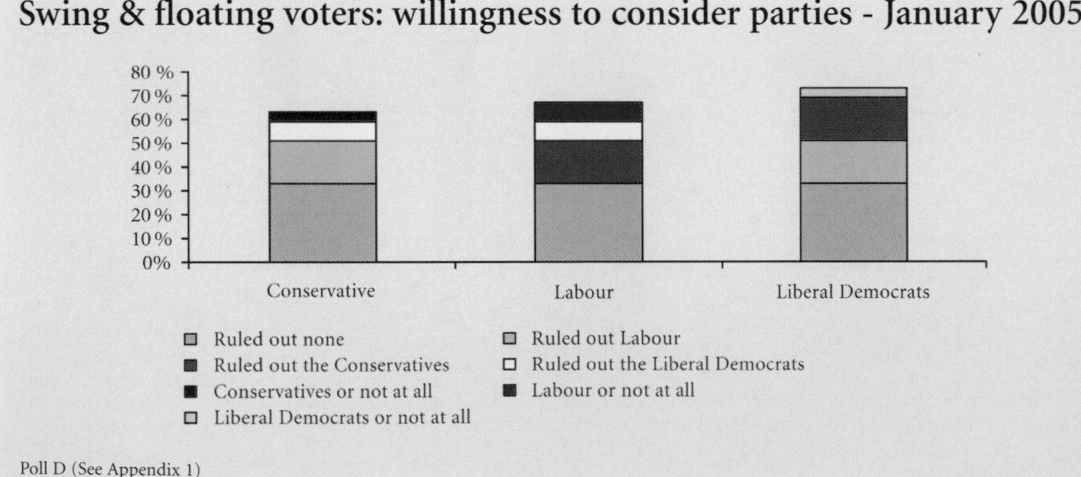

Poll D (See Appendix 1)

ruled out voting for the Liberal Democrats. Altogether, 63% of swing and floating voters were willing to consider the Conservatives, 67% Labour and 73% the Liberal Democrats.

This set of questions revealed some interesting attitudes in particular groups. More 25-44 year-olds (19%) had ruled out voting Conservative than had ruled out voting Labour (14%), and twice as many over 65s (24%) had ruled out Labour as had ruled out the Conservatives. Perhaps more significantly, slightly more ABs had already decided against the Conservatives (22%) than had ruled out Labour, and DEs were more likely to have ruled out Labour (18%) than the Tories (14%).

Tactical Voting

Among those who had decided how to vote there was significant potential for tactical voting, with the Liberal Democrats the likely beneficiaries from both directions. When asked how they would vote if the constituency where they lived was a two-horse race between the Liberal Democrats and the Conservatives, nearly a third of Labour voters (32%) said they would vote Liberal Democrat to stop the Tories. Only 5% of Labour voters said they would vote Conservative to stop the Liberal Democrats, and 45% - a very similar proportion as for the other parties - would vote Labour anyway. 15% said they wouldn't bother to vote at all. Conservatives living in Labour-Liberal Democrat marginals would behave almost identically: 32% would vote Liberal Democrat to stop Labour, 5% the opposite.

While Conservative and Labour supporters inclined to vote tactically would try to defeat each other, Liberal Democrats were inclined to vote against the Conservatives – but not by the same margin as their Labour counterparts. Just over a fifth of Liberal Democrats (21%) said that in a Conservative-Labour marginal they would vote Labour to stop the Tories, but 15% said they would vote for the Conservatives to beat Labour.

Why Won't You Vote Conservative?

People saying they did not currently vote Conservative were more or less evenly divided as to whether they might ever do so. The 48% (34% of all voters) who said they could vote Conservative in the future were invited to agree or disagree with a selection of statements that might have explained their reluctance to support the party at the moment. Clear majorities thought the party was "too dominated by men" (especially among women, 67% of whom agreed, although 52% of men did too), came across as "opportunist, just opposing whatever Labour does and saying whatever they think might be popular" and had "no strong leaders".

This group was then given six different statements about what might make them more likely to vote Conservative in the future. By huge majorities they wanted the party to concentrate on developing policies to improve the NHS and other public services (78%), champion policies to make

What potential Conservatives think of the Tory party

Asked of voters who don't vote Conservative but say they may in the future

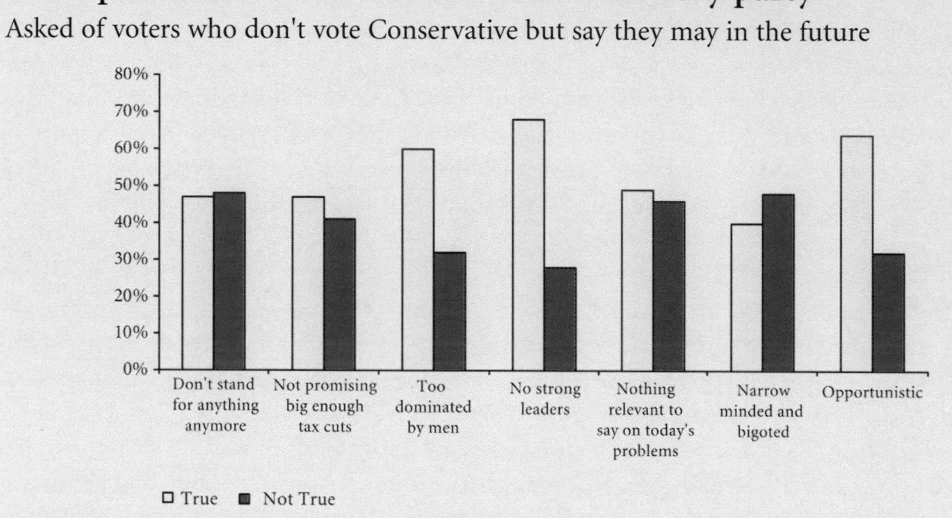

Poll D (See Appendix 1)

What would make them more likely to vote Conservative?

Asked of voters who don't vote Conservative but say they may in the future

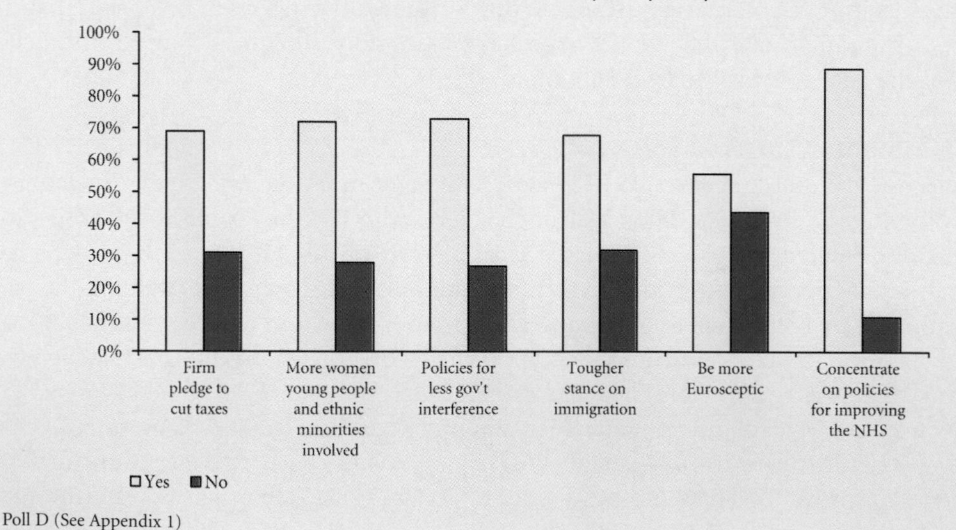

Poll D (See Appendix 1)

government less interfering in how people live their lives (46%), and involve more women, young people and ethnic minorities to make the Conservatives look more like modern Britain (44%). Smaller but still sizeable majorities sought a tougher stance on immigration and asylum (36%) and a specific commitment to tax cuts (38% - though this won overwhelming support among 18-24s, with 81% saying such a policy would make them more likely to vote Conservative); a relatively small margin (12%) favoured a much more sceptical approach to the EU.

What are the Parties Like?

The exercise also explored whether people felt each party had certain positive characteristics. In every case, clear majorities felt the Conservatives lacked the attribute in question. 60% said the party did not share their values; 56% thought the party was not competent and capable; 58% said it did not care about the problems that ordinary people have to deal with, and 63% thought the Conservatives would not deliver what they promised if they were elected. In each case, 35-44 year-olds felt more strongly negative than the population as a whole, disagreeing on each characteristic by four or five points more than the national average.

Only the Conservatives inspired this uniformly negative view. Slim majorities thought Labour was competent and capable (49%-46%) and cared about ordinary people's problems (49%-47%) – a characteristic they also attributed to the Liberal Democrats by a more comfortable margin

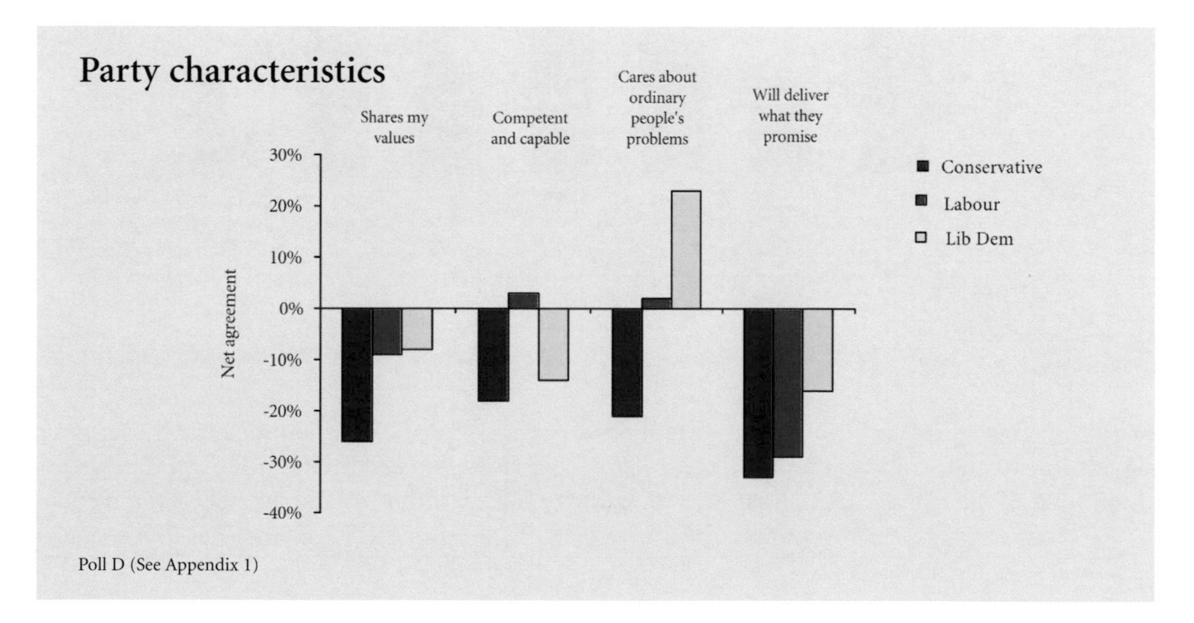

Poll D (See Appendix 1)

(57%-34%). On only one measure did the Conservatives do better than another party: 38% thought they were competent and capable, compared to 37% for the Liberal Democrats.

The research also underlined the extent to which Tony Blair was seen to differ from old Labour. Nearly half of all voters (49%) agreed that "Tony Blair is not like traditional Labour politicians – his values and outlook are closer to what you'd expect from a Conservative than from a Labour prime minister", while 40% did not. Of those that agreed, 41% said this was a good thing, while half disagreed.

Back to the Battleground: The Leaders

In a separate poll[27] we asked voters in the 130 most marginal Labour constituencies in which the Conservatives were second about their views of Tony Blair and Michael Howard.

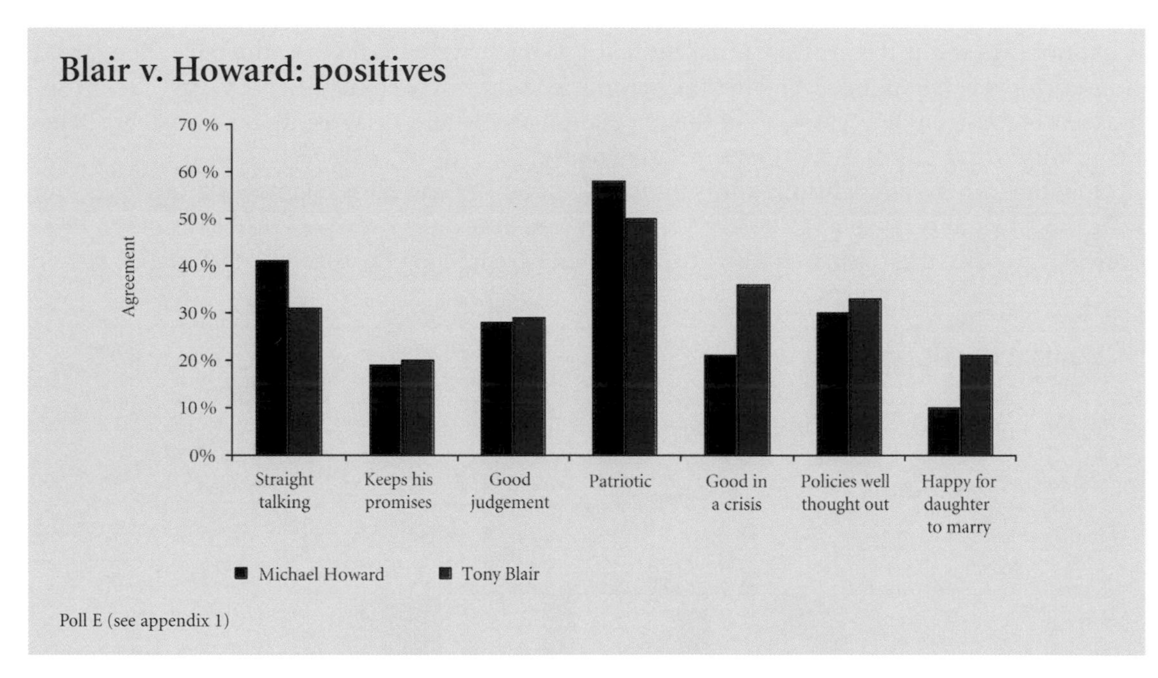

Poll E (see appendix 1)

When asked whether each leader had certain positive characteristics, Mr Howard was ahead only on patriotism and straight talking. The two were closely matched on whether they could be relied upon to keep their promises (neither was thought very likely to do so) and whether, even if their

27 Poll E: see Appendix 1.

policies were not appealing, they were well thought-out (less than a third thought they were in both cases). Mr Blair was the more trusted to be good in a crisis, although more men (41%) than women (32%) thought he displayed this attribute. Mr Howard was also given more credit in this area by men (24%) than women (18%).

However, only just over a fifth of voters would be happy for Mr Blair to marry their daughter if he were younger and single – more than twice as many as would be pleased to walk their offspring down the aisle to Mr Howard.

Blair v. Howard: negatives

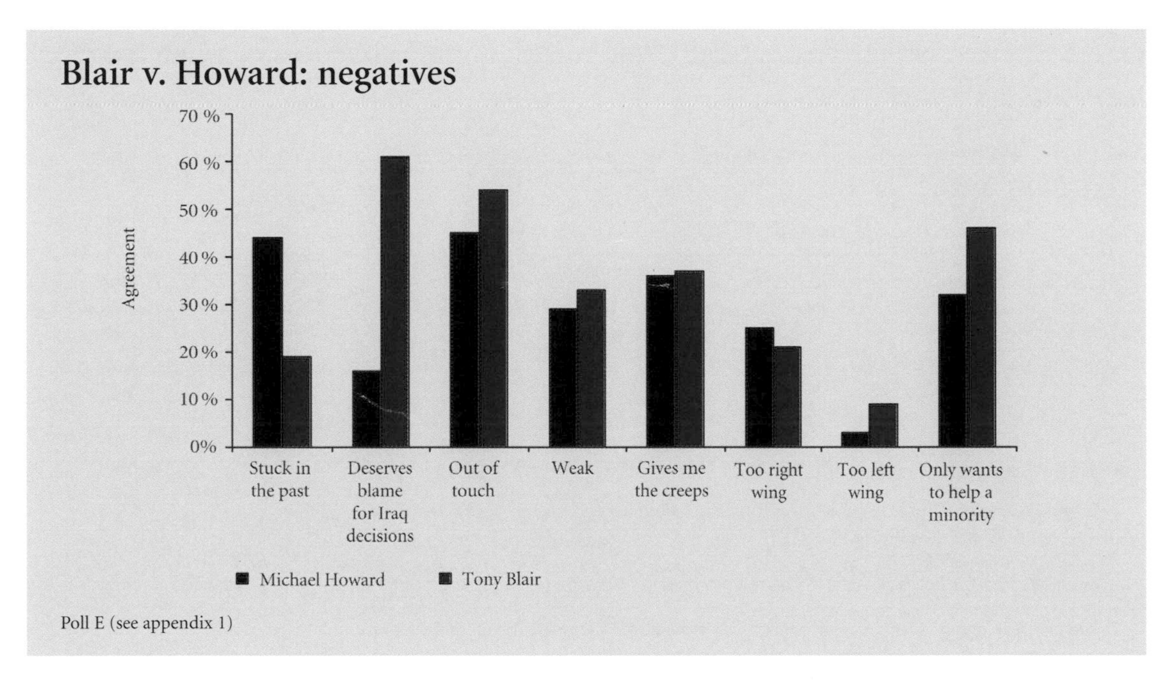

Poll E (see appendix 1)

Apart from the charges of being "stuck in the past" and deserving blame for their decisions over Iraq (in which Mr Howard and Mr Blair respectively had handsome leads), the two leaders were quite similarly regarded. Indeed, Mr Howard only just pipped the prime minister to the title of being most widely considered too right-wing.

Modern Britain, or Why Conservatives are Different

In the 10,000-sample poll, a selection of questions involving statements about Britain today revealed some telling differences in attitude among different types of voter. There was a broad consensus that "Britain is a tolerant country", with 84% agreeing overall – the same proportion that declared themselves "proud to be British".

Rather fewer thought that Britain was "a united country" (62%), but most (69%) agreed that "the diverse mix of races, cultures and religions now found in our society has been good for Britain". Support for this idea ranged from 78% among 25-34 year-olds and 77% among ABs to 57% among those aged 65 and over.

The proportion agreeing that "gay couples should have exactly the same rights as heterosexual couples" (65%) masked differences in view between men (58%) and women (70%), and between the oldest voters (49%) and the youngest (76%). At 57%, Conservative voters were among the least supportive of the proposition.

Do you agree that…

Britain is a tolerant country	84%
I am proud to be British	84%
Britain is a united country	62%
The diverse mix of races, cultures and religions now found in our society has been good for Britain	69%
Gay couples should have exactly the same rights as heterosexual couples	65%
It is not a matter for political parties to express a preference between marriage and couples living together outside marriage	70%
It is not a matter for political parties to express a preference between two-parent families and one-parent families	66%
The single change that would most improve life in Britain today is people being more tolerant of different ethnic groups and cultures	77%
Governments should not use the law to try and change people's private behaviour	65%

Poll D (see appendix 1)

There was little variation from the overall agreement that it is not a matter for political parties to express a preference "between marriage and couples living together outside marriage" (70%), or "between two-parent families and one-parent families" (66%), although younger people and higher social groups were more liberal in both cases. All groups came within a few points of the 77% national level of agreement that "the single change that would most improve life in Britain today is people being more tolerant of different ethnic groups and cultures".

However, two propositions revealed enormous differences in attitude between Conservative voters and the rest of the population – and particularly young people, swing voters and the once staunchly Tory AB social group. First, more than two thirds (67%) of Conservative voters agreed with the proposition "Britain was a better country to live in 20 or 30 years ago" – well above the national average of 55% and miles away from that of younger voters and ABs.

"Britain was a better country to live in 20 or 30 years ago"

All voters	18-24s	ABs	Conservative voters
55%	36%	43%	67%

Poll D (see appendix 1)

The second proposition on which Tories took a strikingly different view to Britain as a whole concerned the prospects of the Conservative Party itself. Only 38% of all voters thought "the Conservative Party is making progress and is on the right track to get back in power before long". Yet 79% of Conservatives thought this was the case. This meant existing Conservative supporters were more than twice as likely to think their party was on course to win an election as the swing voters who would decide whether or not it actually did (40%).

"The Conservative Party is making progress and is on the right track to get back in power before long"

All voters	18-24s	ABs	Conservative voters
38%	33%	35%	79%

Poll D (see appendix 1)

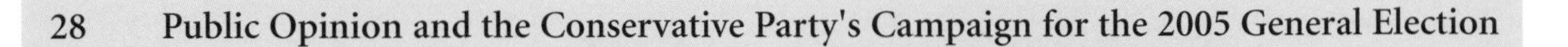

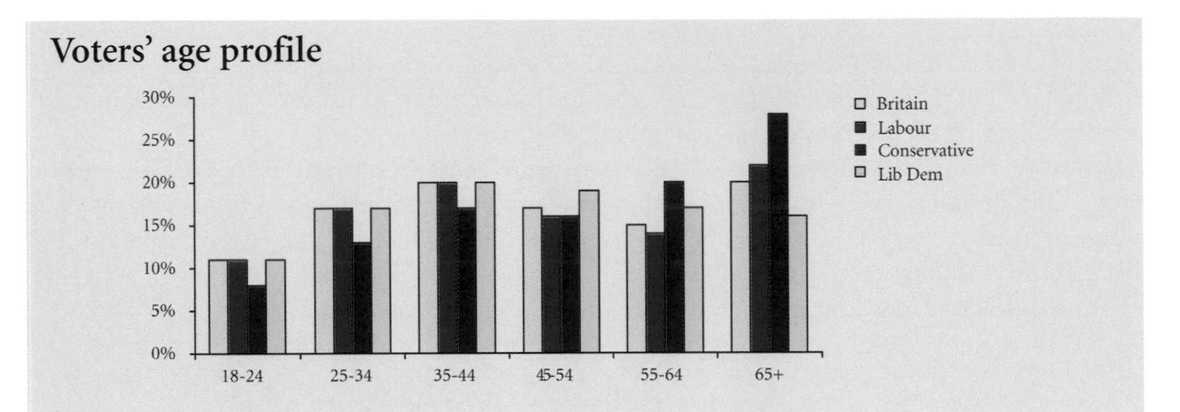
Voters' age profile
30%
25%
20%
15%
10%
5%
0%
18-24
25-34
35-44
45-54
55-64
65+
Britain
Labour
Conservative
Lib Dem

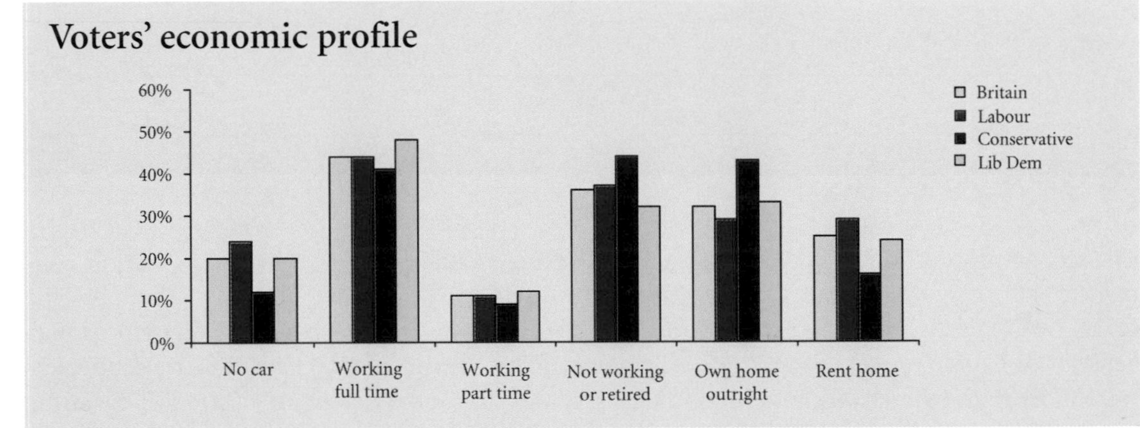
Voters' economic profile
60%
50%
40%
30%
20%
10%
0%
No car
Working full time
Working part time
Not working or retired
Own home outright
Rent home
Britain
Labour
Conservative
Lib Dem

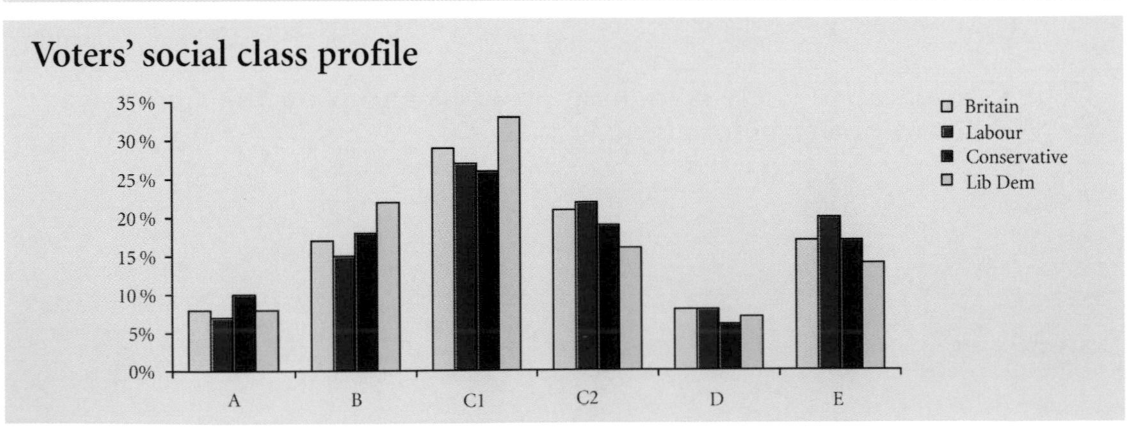
Voters' social class profile
35 %
30 %
25 %
20 %
15 %
10 %
5%
0%
A
B
C1
C2
D
E
Britain
Labour
Conservative
Lib Dem

Differences in attitude between Conservative voters and others on social and cultural questions may be explained in large part by their relative demographic profiles.

While the profile of Labour and Liberal Democrat supporters broadly matched that of Britain, Conservatives relied disproportionately for their support on those aged 55 and over, who were retired or not working, who owned their home outright, and who read the Daily Mail or the Daily Telegraph.

The profile of party support by social class describes a demographic disaster for the Conservatives. In the 1992 general election the Conservatives won 54% of AB votes. Even in 1997, when it won only 31.5% of the vote nationally, the party held 43% of this group. By 2001 this had fallen to 40%. According to this poll, the Conservatives now commanded just 35% of AB support, only 2 points ahead of Labour.

Moreover, as Conservative support among ABs diminished, the size of the AB category relative to the population as a whole grew rapidly. The Conservative Party was holding a shrinking share of an expanding market that had once represented the bedrock of its electoral support.

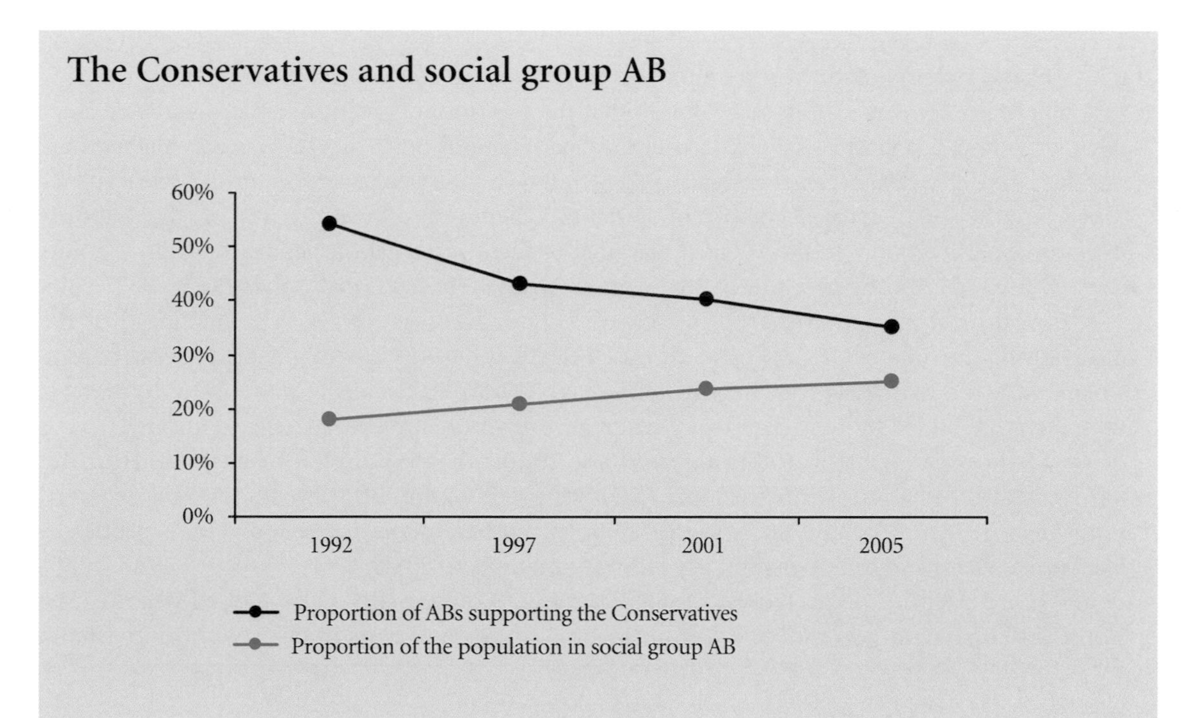

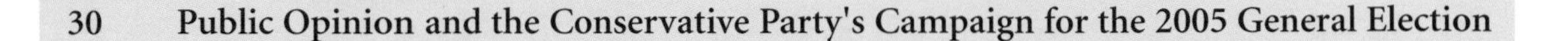

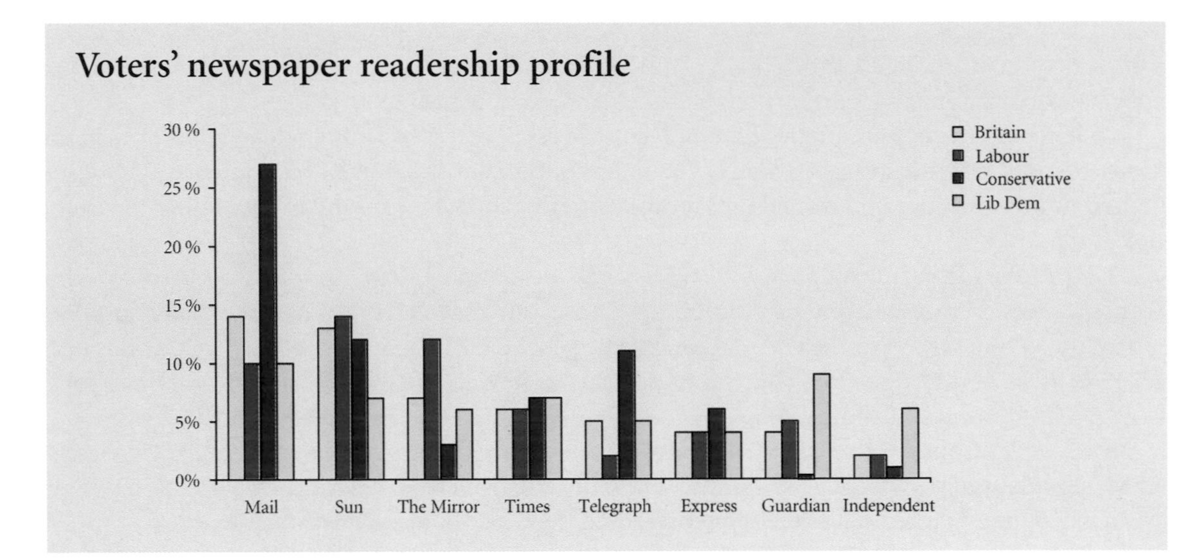

Back to the Battleground: Marginality

A new poll in the 130 key Labour seats[28] found that the gap on this battleground had widened since November, from a 2-point to a 4-point Labour lead, with Labour on 39%. This was only slightly narrower than the 38%-32% national margin YouGov found in their February poll for the Telegraph[29].

However, the poll revealed important variations between different parts of the Labour-Conservative battleground. In the 40 most marginal of these seats, Labour led by less than 2 points (38.9%-37.3%), and in the next tranche the Conservatives were fractionally ahead (35.7%-35.3%). But in the 50 most remote of the 130 marginals, Labour were on 40.9%, 8 points ahead of the Conservatives. The different tranches also expressed clearly differing views on their preference of government, with the marginals with the highest Labour majorities decidedly more likely to prefer a Labour government led by Tony Blair to a Conservative government led by Michael Howard.

This second wave of battleground research also found that expectations had moved further towards victory for Labour. More than half (51%) of voters in the 130 Labour seats now expected Labour to win again locally, up from 49% in November, with the proportion expecting a Conservative victory in their constituency falling from 26% to 23%.

As with voting intention, expectations varied according to marginality. Only 45% of voters in the top 40 Conservative targets expected Labour to hold on in their constituency, with more than a

28 Poll E: see Appendix 1.

29 22-24 February 2005, sample 1,997, published in the Daily Telegraph 25 February 2005

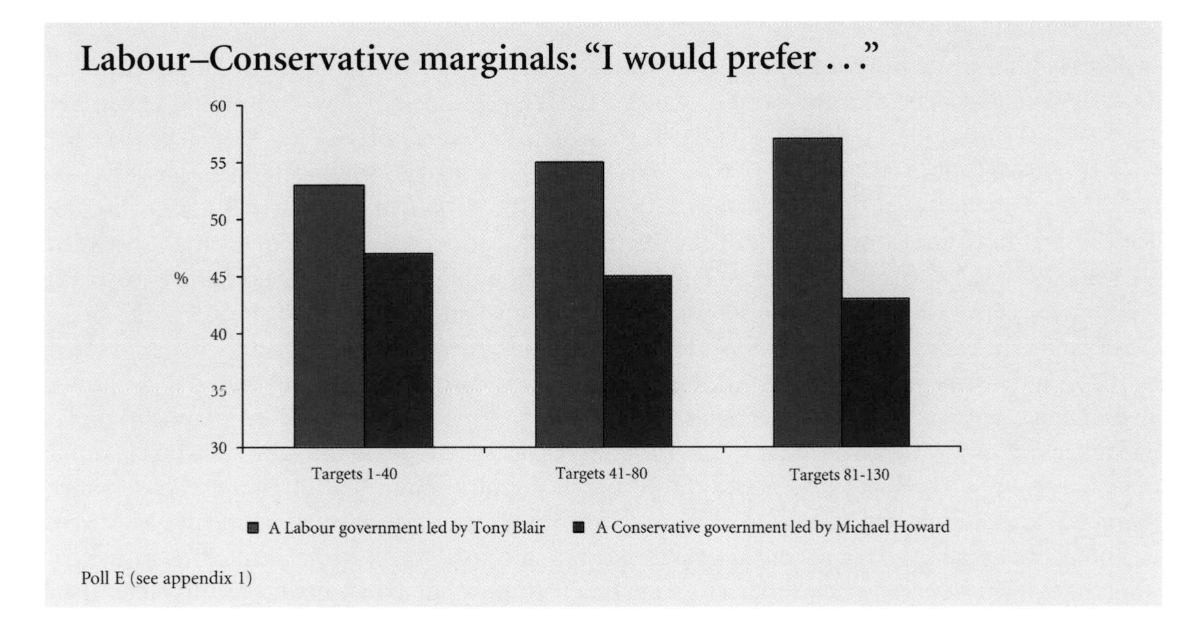

Poll E (see appendix 1)

third (35%) expecting their seat to fall to the Tories. In the next tranche, 48% expected Labour to win, rising to 57% in targets 81-130. 31% expected the Conservatives to win in targets 41 to 80, and only just over a fifth (21%) in the bottom 50.

The Labour government's performance had improved since the autumn in the eyes of battleground voters, and the Conservatives were doing better at providing an alternative. Public estimation of the Liberal Democrats' performance had slipped slightly, but they were still thought to be doing better than the Tories.

How are the parties doing at governing/providing an alternative government?

	November 2004		February 2005	
	Well	Badly	Well	Badly
Labour	42%	55%	45%	50%
Conservatives	24%	68%	30%	63%
Liberal Democrats	41%	31%	40%	46%

Poll A & E (see appendix 1)

There was still little published polling information on the key marginal seats. However, in an analysis[30] of data collected from around 21,000 interviews conducted between July and December 2004, MORI found that in the 50 seats in which Labour had a majority of less than 10% over the Conservatives, Labour still led by 37% to 32%. This represented a swing to the Conservatives of only 0.5% (smaller even than the national swing of 2.7% suggested by the study), meaning the Tories were on course to win only 4 of the 50. In the 78 seats with a Labour majority of between 10% and 20% the swing was greater at 6.5%, but still enough only for the Conservatives to claim another 23 seats – well short of the 103 in which the party had claimed to be ahead.

A Populus poll for the News of the World[31] in January returned to the 202 constituencies surveyed by ICM for the same newspaper the previous June[32]. This exercise found the situation in these seats – all marginals, but not the same selection as that defined by the Conservatives as their battleground – had taken a turn for the worse as far as the Tories were concerned. While the June ICM poll had put the Conservatives 5 points ahead across the 202 seats, Populus found that in Labour-Conservative marginals, Labour now led by 46% to 32%, a gap of 14%. In territory where Conservative MPs were defending marginal seats against the Liberal Democrats, the Tories trailed by a point, 37% to 36%.

Though the Conservatives continued to claim that their position in marginal seats was better than that suggested in national polls – though without alluding again to specific private polling (perhaps because ORB's membership of the British Polling Council, established in November 2004, would have required them to publish details of the results and methodology of any poll which their client put into the public domain). However, this was not supported by the evidence from our extensive research. In the Labour-Conservative battleground, although Labour's lead was fractionally lower than it was nationally, Conservative support remained below its 2001 level of 36%.

Furthermore, given the closeness of the position in the most winnable seats, these findings underlined the risk that the more campaigning resources the Conservatives devoted to the more ambitious battleground seats, the fewer seats they would win in the top half of the target list – and therefore, given the uphill struggle in the tougher targets, the fewer seats they would win overall.

The Story of the Campaign: A Daily Tracking Study

In addition to the 10,000 sample poll, in January 2005 I commissioned a national tracking study[33]. Involving 250 interviews every day for five months – a total of more than 29,000 - this unprecedented project would paint a picture of the unfolding pattern of the election. As well as continu-

30 'Marginal Success?', Mark Gill, MORI, 6 January 2005. See mori.com

31 10-13 January 2005, published in the News of the World 16 January 2005.

32 Conducted 1-3 June 2004, published in the News of the World 6 June 2004.

33 Poll F: see Appendix 1.

ously monitoring the strength of support for parties and views on important policy issues and party attributes, the tracker poll asked, without prompting, what voters had heard the Conservative Party saying and doing from day to day. In this way it was possible to measure the cut-through of Conservative messages and their impact on voting intention and other underlying measures of the party's prospects.

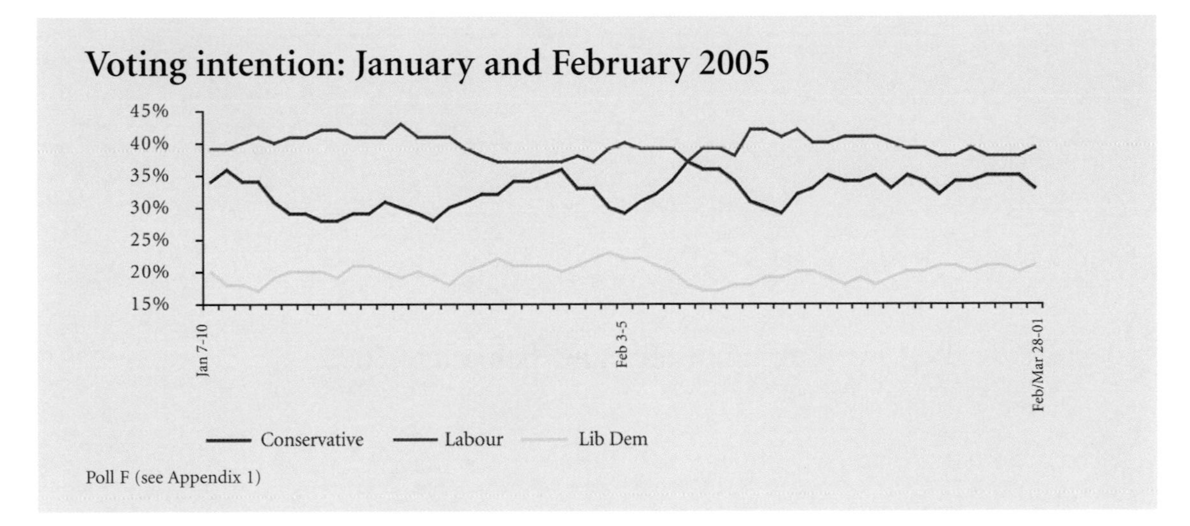

Poll F (see Appendix 1)

At the end of February, each party found itself in a similar position to that in which it began the year. Labour led the Conservatives 39% to 33%, compared to 39%-34% on the first day of the study, with the Liberals on 21%, up one point over the period.

The intervening two months contained a series of peaks and troughs, particularly for the Conservatives whose share of the support fluctuated between 28% and 37%, when they drew level with Labour on February 6-9. At no point during the period did they overtake Labour.

The line representing Conservative Party support is a similar shape to those describing voters' agreement that the party has certain characteristics: that it shares their values, would do a good job in government, has plans to deal with important problems, and stands for action not words.

One of the most striking things about the findings about voters' recall of Conservative messages illustrated a critical fundamental point about political campaigning: how very little of the parties' frenetic activity gets through to people at all. Every day over this period at least two thirds, and often up to 90% of respondents, when asked "has there been anything in the news about what the Conservative Party has been saying or doing that has caught your eye this week, whether on TV

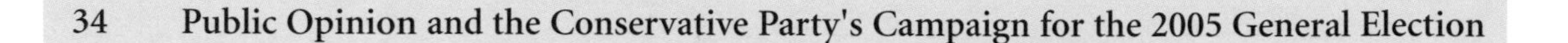

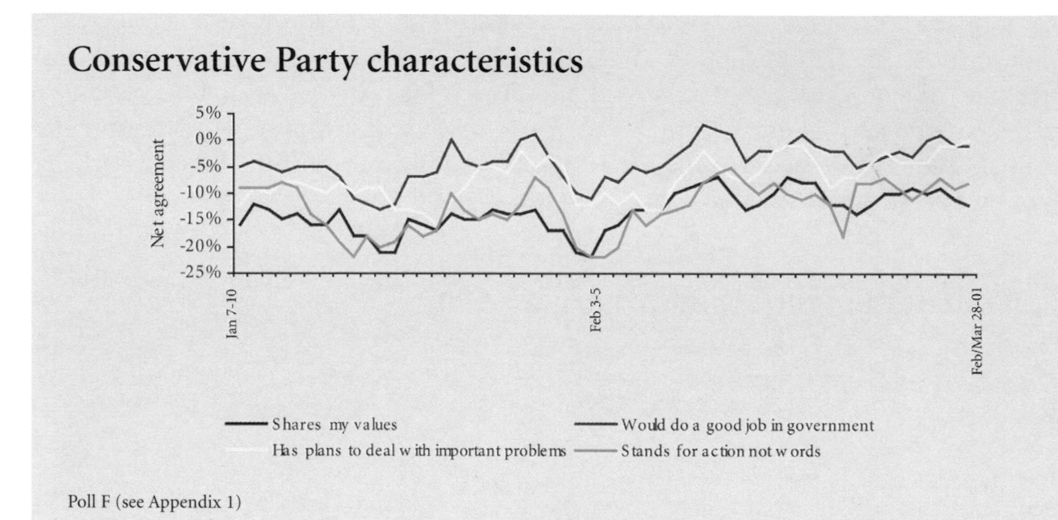

Poll F (see Appendix 1)

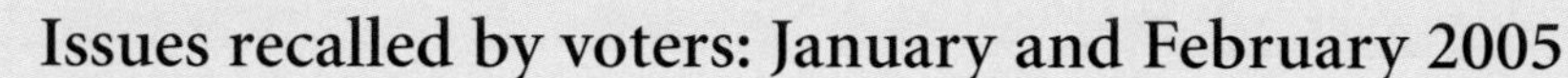

Issues recalled by voters: January and February 2005

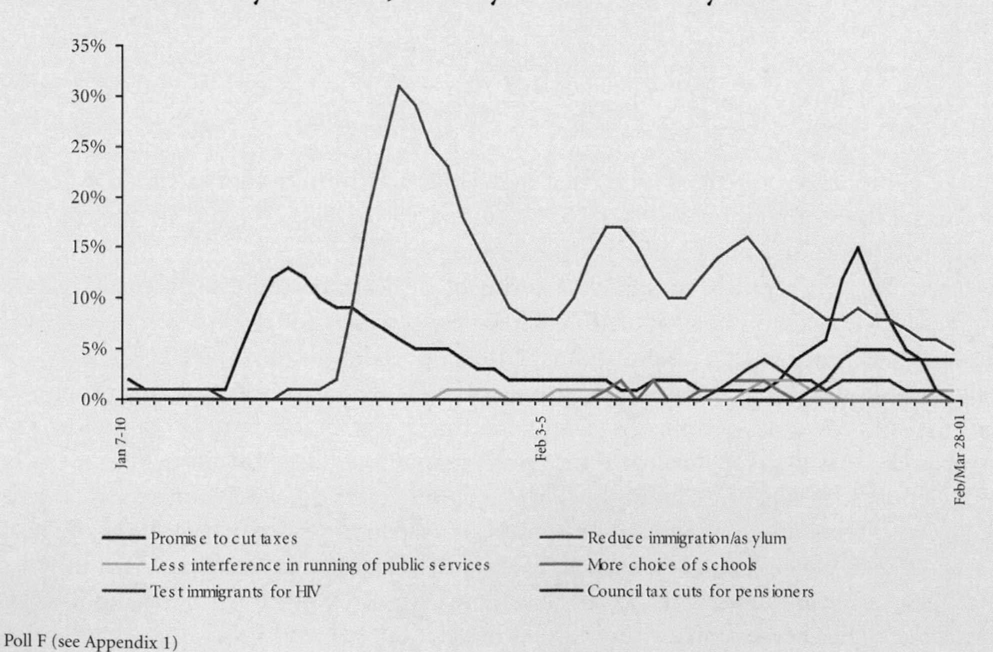

Poll F (see Appendix 1)

or radio or in the papers?" could think of nothing. Even some events that were covered prominently in the news were recalled by almost nobody. Recall for Conservative promises of more police, better value for money, fewer civil servants, less government interference in the running of public services and more choice of schools each peaked at 2% during January and February. The central campaign messages of cleaner hospitals and school discipline peaked at 1% during the period.

Only two Conservative messages became prominent in the public mind: the party's promises to cut taxes and to limit immigration and asylum.

Proposed tax cuts were the only issue to have been recalled by at least 1% of voters every day during the life of the tracker poll, and the first to make any kind of impact on the public in 2005. In the third week in January, voter recall of the Conservatives talking about tax cuts rose from 1% to 13%. The issue fell steadily back until the end of February, when it again rose quickly within a few days to a high of 15%.

These two peaks followed identifiable news events. On 17 January the Conservatives published the findings of the 'James Review', a commission led by the businessman David James which identified potential savings in government spending, which the party used as the basis for its promise of lower taxes and better value for money. On 21 February, Michael Howard announced his proposal to give council tax discounts of up to £500 to pensioners aged over 65. (Although this announcement achieved relatively high recall in itself, it is likely that many voters took it to reinforce a general message of tax cuts).

The first extraordinary spike in recall of Conservative messages about asylum and immigration can be traced back to Michael Howard's heavily trailed and controversial announcement on 24 January that a Conservative government would set an annual limit to immigration, including a quota for asylum seekers – a message which he reinforced with another speech four days later. The subject's return to the political agenda with the government's plan to introduce a points system for new immigrants (7 February) and the Conservatives' proposal to test migrants for diseases including HIV and TB (15 February) may account for the subsequent rises in recall.

As well as measuring the extent to which voters noticed different Conservative messages, the tracking study was able to identify what impact these messages had on perceptions of the party and its policies and, ultimately, their inclination to vote for it.

As the graph shows, the only issue on which the Conservatives enjoyed a clear and consistent lead over Labour was asylum and immigration. The two clear peaks – 24-27 January and 15-18 February – correspond precisely with the peaks for Conservative messages on those subjects.

The first peak in recall of tax messages did not bring a corresponding rise in the proportion of voters thinking the Conservatives were the best party on "the amount of tax ordinary people pay".

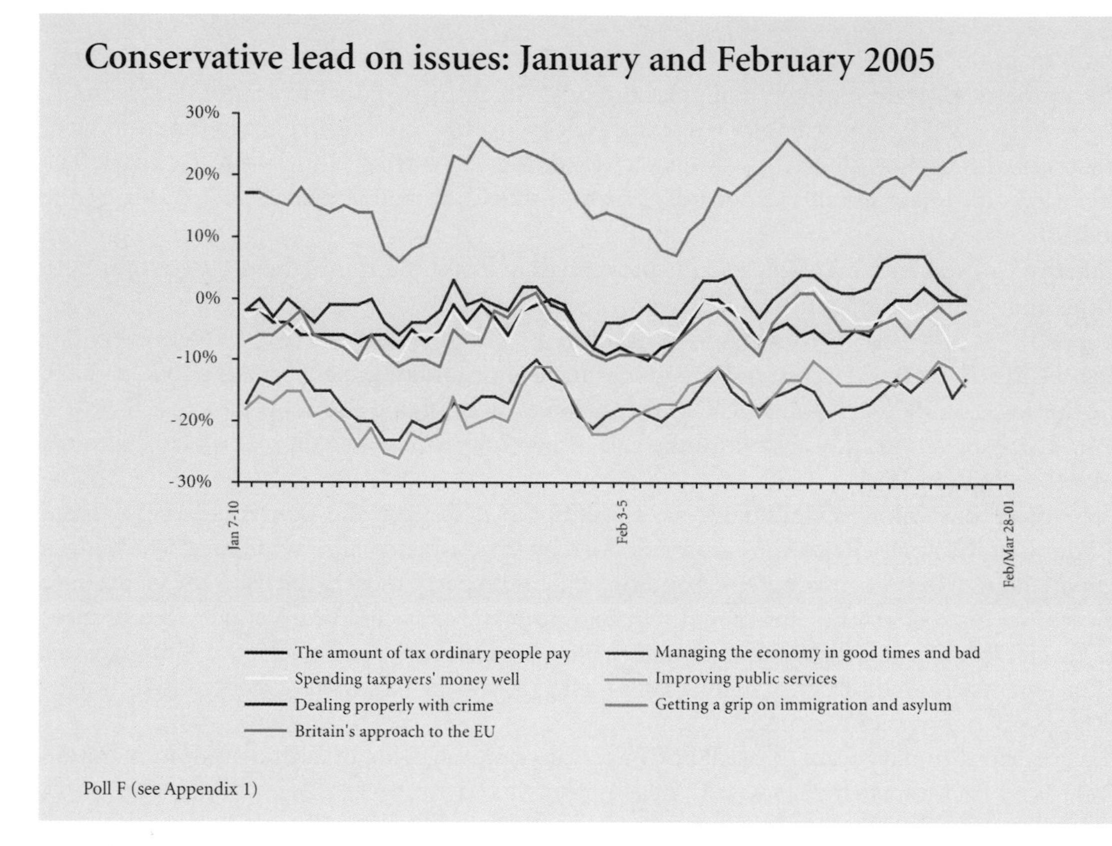

Poll F (see Appendix 1)

On 17-20 January, when 13% of voters recalled hearing the Conservatives talking about the subject, Labour still led on the issue by 6% - a similar proportion to that in the days preceding and following. However, on 22-25 February, when recall of tax messages reached 15%, Labour's lead on the subject fell to 2%, and in the following days the Conservatives drew level.

It is as striking as the Conservative lead on immigration that in two critical areas - improving public services, and managing the economy in good times and bad – the party was not even close to challenging the government.

The only one of four positive attributes with which more people ever agreed than disagreed applied to the party – and then only for a few days at a time - was that it "would do a good job in government". Rather fewer generally thought that the party "has plans to deal with the important problems", and clear majorities consistently disagreed that the party "shares my values" or "stands for action not words".

Conservative attributes: Net agreement January and February 2005

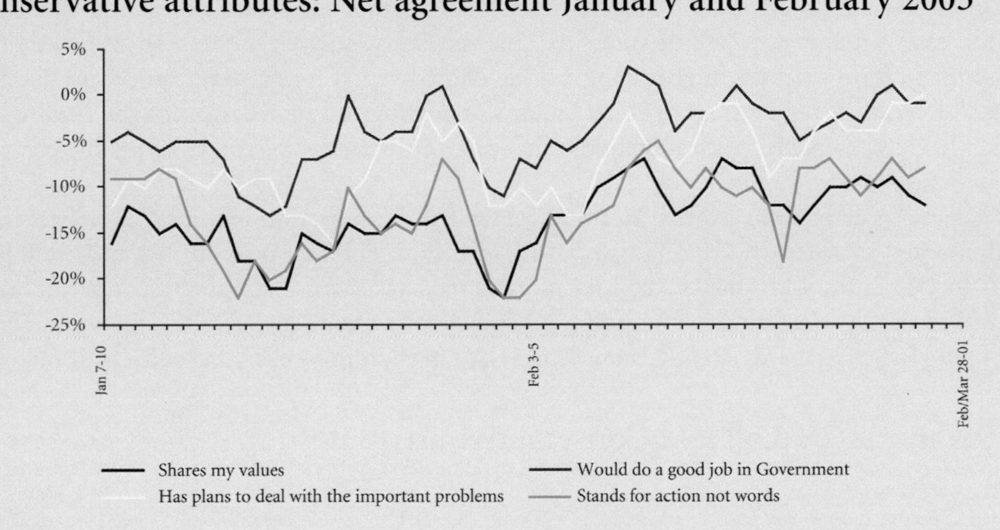

Poll F (see Appendix 1)

Conservative voting intention, message recall & lead on tax

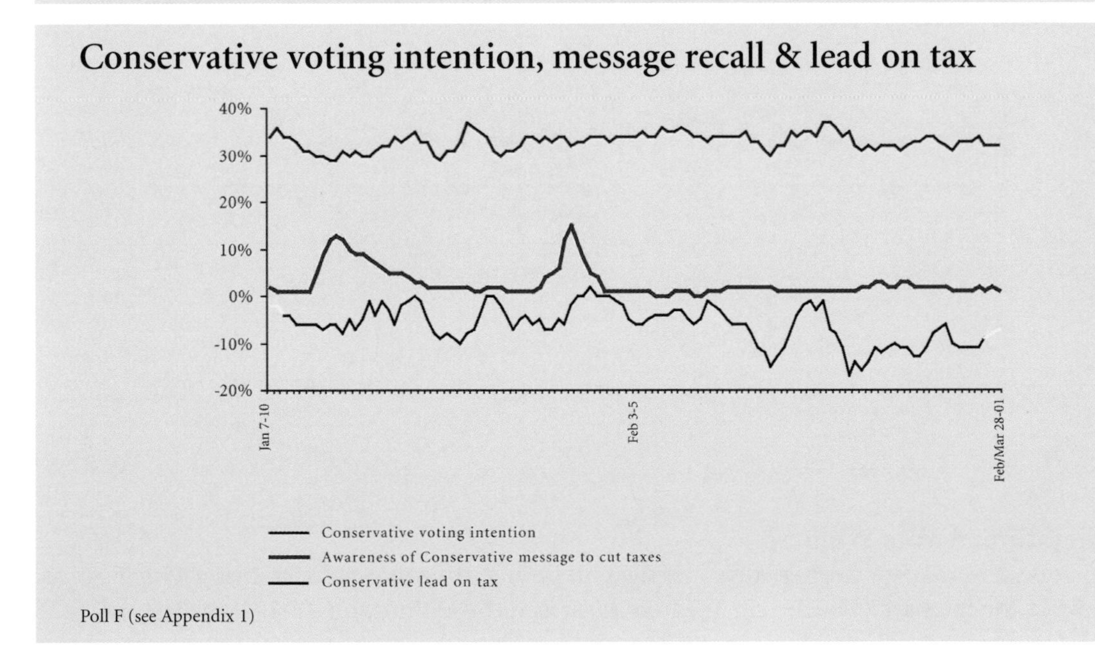

Poll F (see Appendix 1)

Spikes in "would do a good job in government" and "stands for action not words" coincide with an increase in the proportion of voters naming the Conservatives as the best party on all issues, although in most cases this higher approval was short-lived. It may also be significant that the first peak for recall of tax messages (17-20 January, following the publication of the findings of the James Review) coincided with a dip in the already low proportion of voters saying the party shared their values.

Peaks in recall of Conservative messages on tax and immigration did not generally correspond with marked increases in Conservative voting intention. The first peak for tax, on 17-20 January, actually coincided with one of the lowest levels of Conservative support recorded between the New Year and the election: 29%, 12 points behind Labour. On 22-25 February, the second tax peak, Tory support at 32% was slightly lower than it had been in the weeks preceding and following.

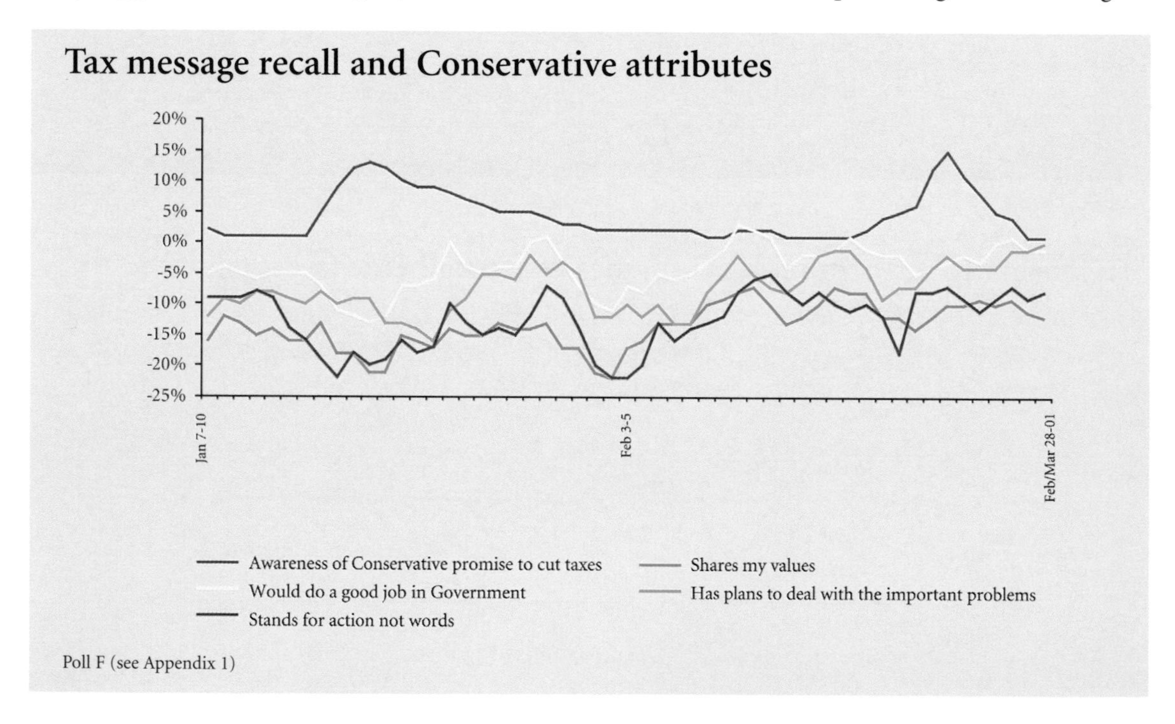

Immigration: A Vote Winner?

The first peak in recall of Conservative messages on immigration also failed to bring with it a peak in support for the party, which remained on 32%, as did the third, on 15-18 February, when it

Conservative voting intention, message recall and lead on immigration

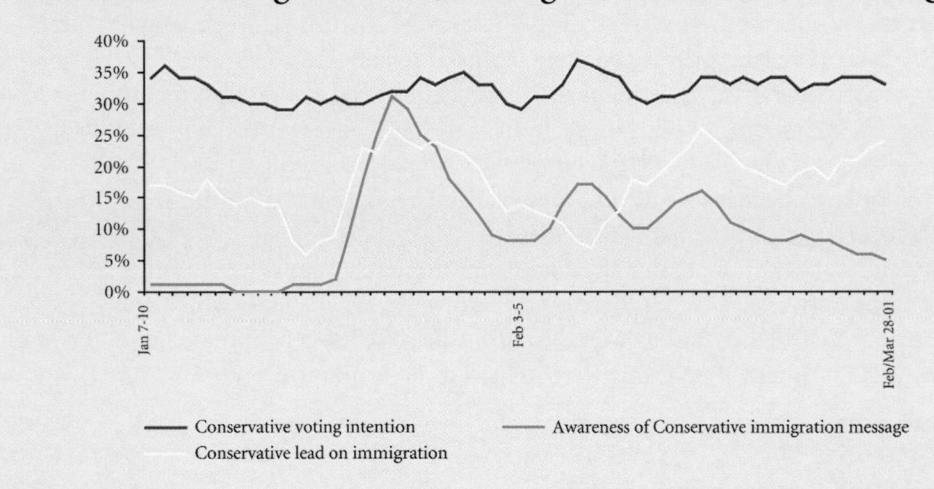

Poll F (see Appendix 1)

Immigration message recall, Conservative attributes

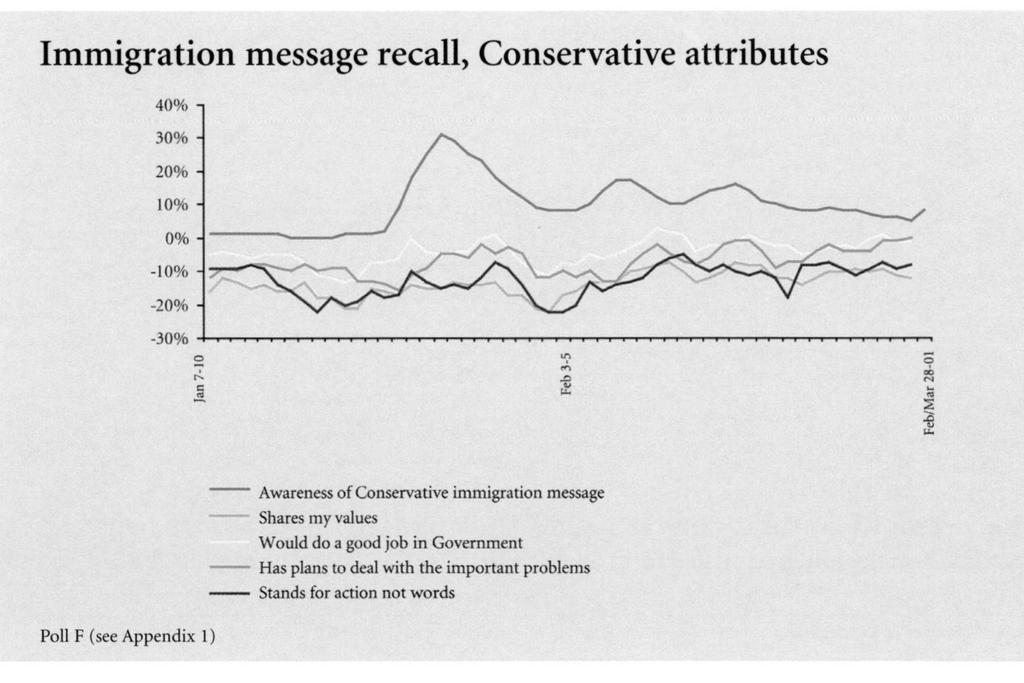

Poll F (see Appendix 1)

trailed Labour by 40% to 34%. However, the second peak, on 6-9 February, coincided with the Conservatives tying with Labour on 37%, their highest level recorded between January and polling day. Even so, Conservative support immediately began to decline (and within a few days had fallen back to 30%, once again putting the party 12 points behind Labour) even though recall of immigration messages remained relatively high. In fact, the Conservatives' high point for voting intention, 6-9 February, coincided with a trough in their lead on immigration.

This lack of linkage between recall of immigration messages and voting intention may be explained by our series of polls in battleground seats.

In early November 2004, more than half of voters in these seats considered immigration one of the four most important issues facing the country. However, when asked which four issues were the most important facing their family, immigration was much less prominent in voters' minds. Meanwhile the NHS, crime and pensions were judged to be important on both counts.

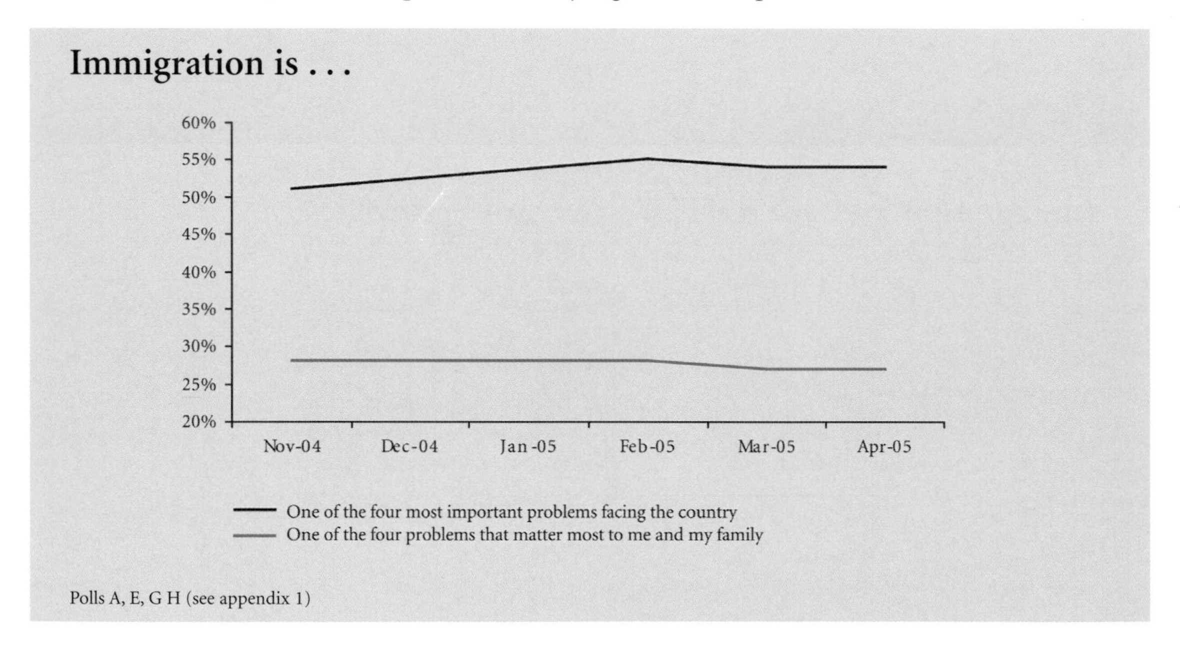

Polls A, E, G H (see appendix 1)

This picture persisted throughout the campaign[34]. The health service increased in importance to voters both nationally and personally, from a very high base, as did crime and, in the last month,

34 Polls A, E, G, H: see Appendix 1.

pensions and social security. Despite the huge attention paid to the subject, as far as their families were concerned voters actually regarded immigration as one of the least important of the prominent issues throughout the election.

After Michael Howard's policy announcement on 24 January Peter Kellner of YouGov noted that although the policy was popular, "unless public attitudes to the parties change radically between now and the general election, the impact of Mr Howard's words will be, at most, to help his party gain, or retain, a handful of seats they might otherwise lose. The impact is not nearly enough to propel him into Downing Street…By stressing immigration, Mr Howard seems more likely to shore up his existing support than to win large numbers of converts".[35]

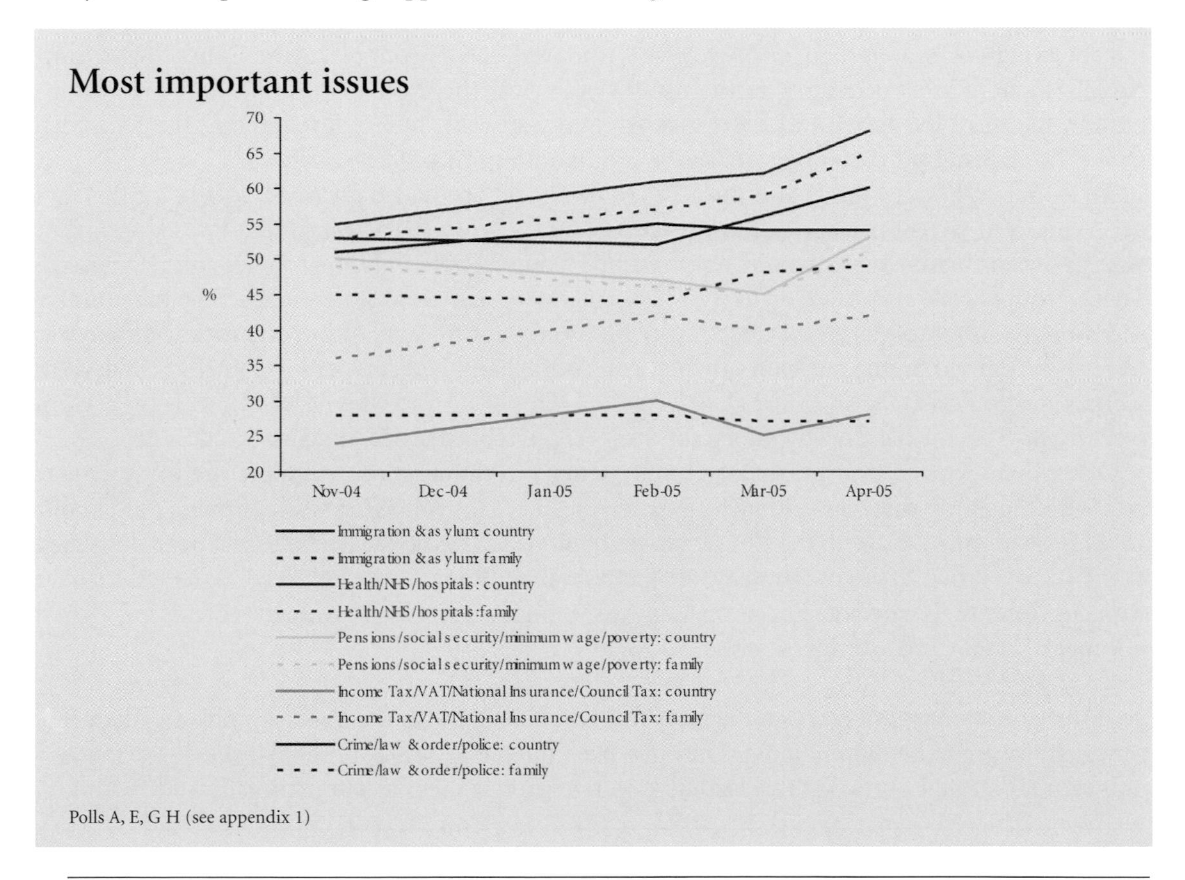

Polls A, E, G H (see appendix 1)

35 'Can the Tories win votes on immigration?', 1 February 2005. See yougov.co.uk.

Since immigration was perhaps a natural Conservative issue, and certainly one on which the party held a clear lead, the strategy behind adopting it as a central campaign theme must have been to increase its salience – to turn it into an issue on which large numbers of people would decide how to vote. The evidence is that the party never achieved this aim. Though the Conservatives undoubtedly succeeded in raising the issue's profile, they did not make it matter more. The public heard the message and largely supported the policy, but were not persuaded that immigration was something that should sway their vote.

In fact there is evidence that the Conservatives' focus on immigration actually cost them support. As Mary Ann Sieghart observed in The Times[36] in March, the people the Conservatives need to woo back if they are to win an election "are not socially conservative, elderly or working class folk, but younger, more urban, middle classes" who were actively put off by the Conservative campaign. She noted that according to the paper's polls over the preceding month, in which immigration had featured heavily, Conservative support had risen by 5 points among the DE social classes but fallen 4 points among ABs and 8 points among C2s.

An earlier poll on the subject for the News of the World[37] provided further evidence for this theory. While 50% of ABs had agreed that "Britain should welcome all new immigrants as long as they pass strict tests to make sure they are able to support themselves", only 36% of C2s and DEs agreed. These groups were also twice as likely (13% and 14%) as ABs (7%) to agree that the country should have an "absolute closed-door policy on immigration". Smaller but significant differences were also recorded on the question of whether or not Britain had accepted its fair share of asylum seekers and couldn't take any more at all (ABs 36%, DEs 58%) and whether the number of asylum seekers was a major reason why public services were overburdened (ABs 32%, C2DEs 56%).

Other than existing Conservatives, a tough policy on immigration was therefore likely to play best with the group that was least likely ever to vote Tory (the following week Populus put Labour 18% ahead among DEs, with the Conservatives on 27%[38]). This approach has often been described as the Conservative "core vote strategy"; in fact, it was anything but. When the Conservatives have won elections, their core vote has comprised ABs, women, aspirational younger voters, and a good number of public sector professionals.

So if the Conservatives hoped that the New Year would bring with it a transformation in their fortunes, they were to be disappointed. They had been unable to rise from the flatline of the January poll rating that had outlived three leaders; voters regarded them as opportunistic and lacking in

36 The Times, 25 March 2005.

37 Conducted by Populus 27-28 January 2005, published in the News of the World 30 January 2005, sample 1,019.

38 Conducted 4-6 February 2005, published in The Times 8-10 February 2005, sample 1,518.

leadership; they were not seen to share most people's values or to stand for action rather than words; and although they quickly succeeded in building a clear lead over Labour on immigration, the issue was not moving votes in sufficient numbers to have a decisive effect on voting intention. And on the Conservatives' chosen battleground, Labour was holding its own on all but the most vulnerable territory.

Chapter Three

Drilling Down

Having benchmarked and tracked changes in voters' attitudes in the seats the Conservatives had defined as the electoral battleground, I commissioned research to probe further into a selection of different constituencies at various points on the party's target list.

Polls were conducted between the end of February and the end of April in a dozen target seats[39], each with a sample of 1,500 - more than is usual even for national polls. The research revealed some stark contrasts in the party's standing and prospects in the different constituencies, all of which it needed to win to return to government together with many more seats beyond those in the range.

The polls showed the Conservatives ahead in five of the seats, Labour ahead in five, and a dead heat in two. While this represented some improvement in Tory fortunes, this was usually due more to the falling popularity of Labour than to any marked increase in Conservative support: across the twelve seats, while Labour's support had declined by an average of nearly 6% since the 2001 election, the Conservative share had risen by only 0.66%. Meanwhile, the Liberal Democrats found themselves 2.75% ahead of their 2001 position, and Others had advanced by 2.42%.

As had been the case in our earlier polls across the whole battleground, the swing to the Conservatives was generally greater in the seats with the lowest Labour majorities. In Bexleyheath & Crayford, where the poll found a 7-point swing to the Conservatives, Labour were defending a majority of only 3.6%. But in Wirral West, the safest Labour seat of the twelve, Populus found a 0.5% swing from the Conservatives to Labour. And in Dartford, with a Labour majority of 7.4%, the Conservatives were still behind having achieved only a 2.5% swing. These findings again suggested that the Tory strategy of targeting the whole battleground might be counterproductive. While constituencies within easy reach looked set to fall, the more ambitious seats looked unattainable and progress in the ones in between was less than the party might have hoped.

39 Peterborough, Bristol West, Wirral West, High Peak, Kettering, Northampton South, Hammersmith & Fulham, Bexleyheath & Crayford, Gillingham, Dartford, The Wrekin and Wimbledon. Poll I: see Appendix 1.

However, the poll revealed some potential for the Labour vote to fall further, particularly where the Conservatives were ahead or level. When Labour voters were asked whether they might decide not to vote at all out of disillusionment with Tony Blair or the government, between 17% and 35% said that they "definitely" or "may" consider doing so.

This inclination among Labour voters to withhold their support was only partly mitigated by the fact that they lived in a marginal constituency. When reminded that their seat was likely to be a close race between Labour and the Conservatives, less than a third of Labour supporters who had considered not voting said the fact would make them more likely to vote after all. While there was some variation between seats, in all cases more than half (and in two cases more than two thirds) of disillusioned Labour voters said the marginality of their constituency would make no difference to the likelihood of their turning out to vote.

Liberal Democrat supporters were reminded that the election in their constituency was expected to be a close two-horse race between Labour and the Conservatives, and asked how this would affect their voting intention, if at all. (This question did not apply in Bristol West, where the Liberal Democrats and the Conservatives had been in close contention for second place in 2001, theoretically making the constituency a three-horse race). Around three quarters said that the relative prospects of the parties would make no difference and they would vote for the Liberal Democrats anyway, but the remainder were quite equally divided between voting Conservative, voting Labour and not voting at all.

Conservative voters expected their party to win in all but one of the constituencies polled. In seven of the seats Conservatives declared, sometimes by a wide margin, that the Tories would also win the election nationally, putting Michael Howard in Downing Street.

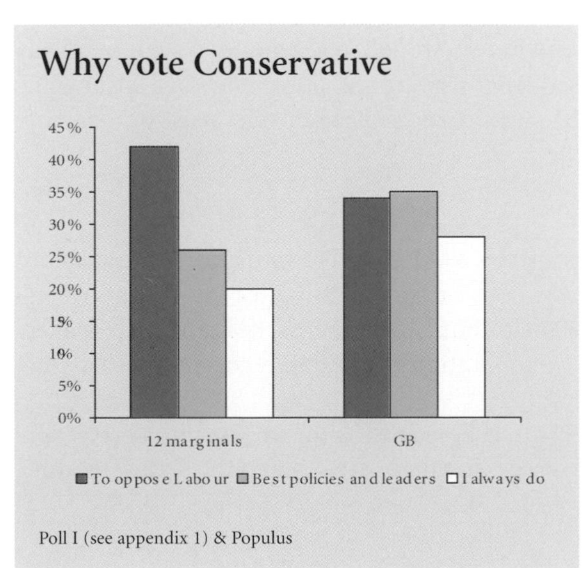

Poll I (see appendix 1) & Populus

We also asked Conservative voters in these seats what their main reason was for voting as they would. They were given three options: "I disapprove of the Labour government and the Conservatives are the main opposition to it"; "The Conservatives have the best policies and leaders overall"; and "I always vote Conservative". (They were also offered the option of answering 'none of the above' or 'don't know'.)

In each of the twelve marginals, opposition to the Labour government was the most common reason for voting Conservative, with only just over a quarter of those intending to vote Tory saying they would do so because the party had the best policies and leaders.

The findings suggest that Conservative voters in these marginal seats were more likely to be motivated by opposition to Labour than those in Britain as a whole. A Populus poll for The Times conducted at the beginning of March[40] found that those intending to vote Conservative were fractionally more likely to do so for positive reasons than to vote against the government, while more than a quarter would do so out of habit.

This series of individual constituency polls suggested that the Conservatives' local campaigns had made some progress since the autumn polls of the 164 battleground seats, and provided some evidence that the main parties were moving away from traditional local campaigning methods towards targeted direct mail. While 19% of voters in the twelve marginals had now received a personally addressed letter from the Conservatives and 18% from Labour, still only 7% said that one or both parties had knocked on their door. Leaflets remained the most popular form of local contact, though, with between a third and half of all households having received literature from one or both parties.

Less clear, at this stage, was the extent to which these local campaigns were likely to affect the outcome of the election. In the five seats in which the Conservatives were ahead, they had delivered the most literature in four, written the most personally addressed letters in four, and knocked on the most doors in one. In the five where Labour led, they had delivered the most literature in none, knocked on the most doors in one and written the most letters in two.

Neither did there seem at this stage to be much correlation between contact rates and swing. The biggest swings, in Bexleyheath & Crayford and Peterborough, corresponded with relatively low rates of literature delivery, personally addressed letter writing and door knocking. Meanwhile some of the most heavily canvassed and leafleted constituencies were at that stage not moving towards the Conservatives.

The Leaders: Bad and Worse?

The polls included a comprehensive appraisal of attitudes to Michael Howard and Tony Blair, and the parties themselves, among voters in key seats. As in our earlier polls, in most cases voters rejected positive statements and agreed with negative ones about both the parties and their leaders (albeit by different margins in different places), corroborating the frequent complaint that elections are a matter of choosing the lesser of two evils.

Across the twelve seats, voters disagreed that "Michael Howard has the personality and leadership qualities needed in a prime minister" by an average margin of 10%, and only just over a third

40 4-6 March 2005, published in The Times 8-12 March 2005.

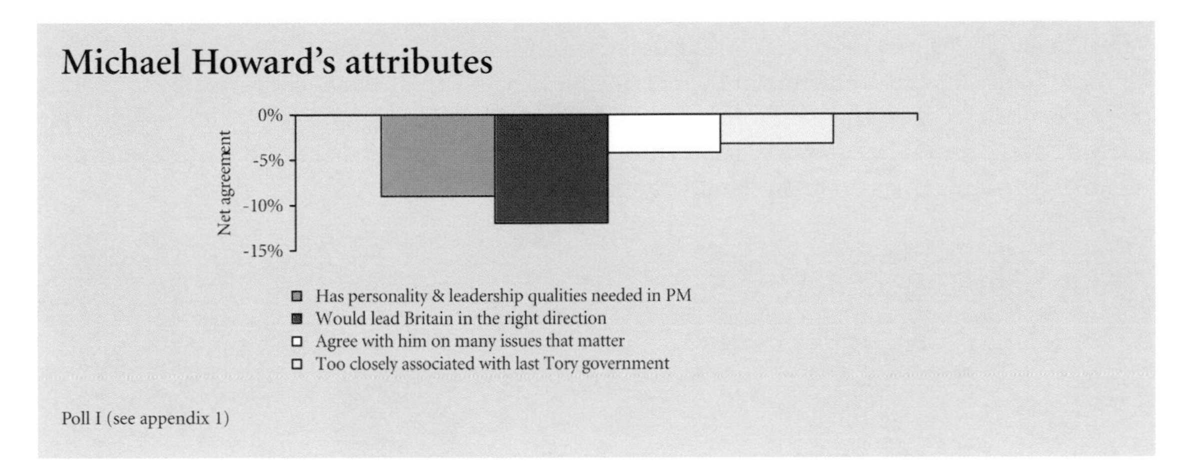

Michael Howard's attributes

Poll I (see appendix 1)

thought he "would lead Britain in the right direction", with 50% disagreeing. Of the suggested positive attributes, "I agree with Michael Howard on many of the issues that matter most to me" gained the most support, with 41% endorsing the statement. Even so, more people disagreed, and the proposition was rejected by a margin of 4%. One positive note for Mr Howard from the exercise was that most voters did not seem inclined to hold his role in John Major's government against him. While 41% thought he was "too closely associated with the last Tory government to be a credible leader now", they were outnumbered by 3%.

Views of Mr Howard were not consistent across the twelve constituencies. In many cases voters in seats where the Conservatives were ahead had a less negative view of him than in those where Labour was holding on, but there were some glaring exceptions. Voters in Hammersmith & Fulham, where the poll found a 3-point Conservative lead, were among the most negative in their opinion of the Conservative leader. Majorities of 15% in the west London seat felt he did not have the requisite personality and leadership qualities for a prime minister and disagreed with him on many important issues, and by a margin of 18% they thought he would lead Britain in the wrong direction. Meanwhile Dartford, where Labour were still ahead, was more favourable to Mr Howard on each question than the twelve as a whole had been.

If anything, voters in this selection of seats thought even less of the prime minister than they did of Mr Howard. Again, they rejected all the positive propositions about Mr Blair and accepted the critical one, but by much higher margins than for his opponent.

A majority of 16% felt Mr Blair was not leading Britain in the right direction (rising to 32% in Bexleyheath & Crayford – though the margin was as low as 4% in The Wrekin and only 7% in Northampton South, where the parties were tied, and 9% in Tory-leaning Hammersmith &

Fulham). By a 17% margin voters did not agree with Mr Blair on many of the issues that matter most to them – four times the margin of disagreement with Mr Howard. They rejected by a decisive 24% majority the proposition that "because Tony Blair has a young family he understands many of the pressures faced by ordinary people", but agreed by a 10% margin that the prime minister "has become arrogant and no longer cares what voters think".

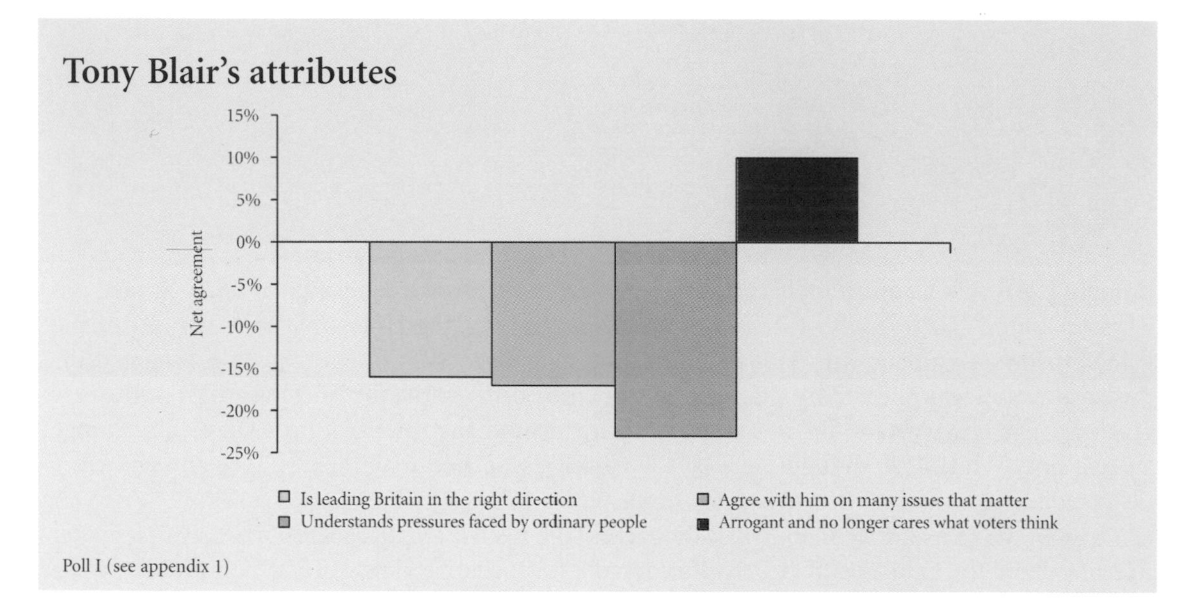

Poll I (see appendix 1)

These findings presented an interesting insight into how voters saw the election, and had implications for the Conservatives' campaign strategy. While neither leader emerged from the exercise with much credit, many voters had evidently taken a firmly negative view of Mr Blair, even in seats that Labour looked on course to hold.

A series of separate national polls confirmed the point. In March, ICM[41] found a third of voters saying they "much prefer" Tony Blair to Michael Howard, with a further 18% saying they preferred Mr Blair "on balance" – a total of 51%. Only 36% preferred Mr Howard to Mr Blair, including 21% who "much prefer" the Conservative leader.

A Populus survey for The Times shortly afterwards[42] found that only a third of voters in Britain thought Mr Blair had been a good prime minister overall. However, less than a quarter would pre-

41 Conducted 18-20 March 2005, published in the Guardian 22 March 2005, sample 1,005.

42 Conducted between 1-3 April 2005, published in The Times 5-7 April 2005.

fer to see Mr Howard in Downing Street - a proportion which had actually declined over the previous 14 months[43].

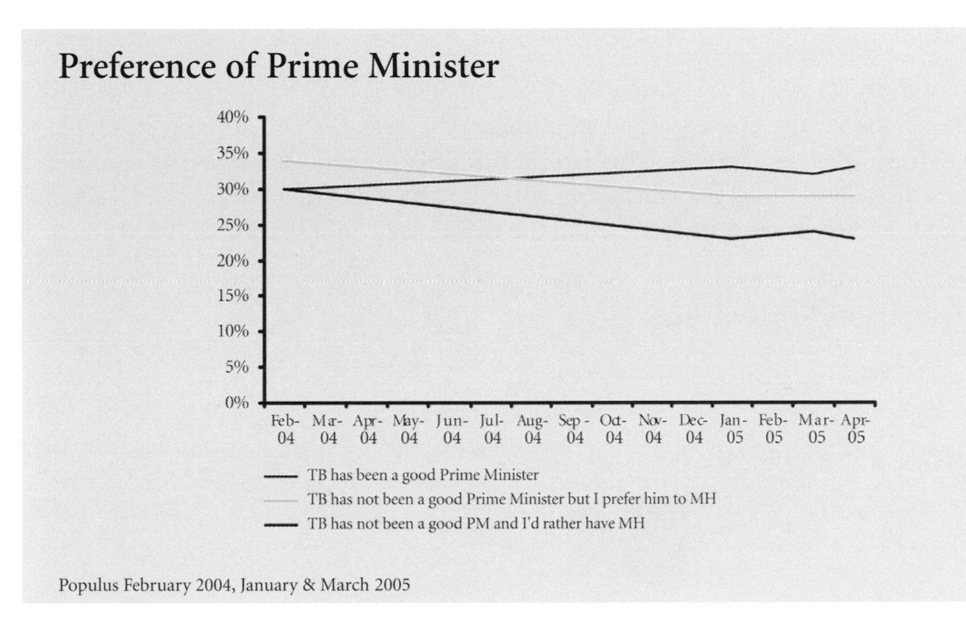

Populus February 2004, January & March 2005

These results, combined with a steady Labour lead in national opinion polls, might have suggested that attacks on Mr Blair, even if they succeeded in further reducing the proportion of people thinking he had been a good prime minister, were unlikely to translate into greater support for the Conservatives. While no more than a third thought at any point that Mr Blair had been a good prime minister overall, those who thought he had not but preferred him to Mr Howard always outnumbered those who preferred Mr Howard. Voters were going to need persuading that they should want to see Michael Howard in Number 10 – and it was already evident that dissatisfaction with Mr Blair was not going to be a good enough reason.

The Parties: Bad and Not So Bad

As far as voters in the twelve marginals were concerned, the Conservative Party itself was still not a particularly appealing sight. By a majority of 13% they agreed that "the Conservatives seem to be stuck in the past and don't seem to be in touch with what life is like in modern Britain". Not

43 Populus polls conducted 6-8 February 2004, published in The Times 10-11 February 2004; 7-9 January 2005, published in The Times 11-13 January 2005; 4-6 March 2005, published in The Times 8-12 March 2005.

surprisingly, the highest net agreement with this proposition was found in the seats where Labour was ahead and vice versa. However, in two of the Conservative-leaning seats, Kettering and Peterborough, net agreement that the Tories were stuck in the past and out of touch was higher than in the average of the twelve.

Voters in two of the seats with a Tory lead – Bexleyheath & Crayford and Kettering – were tied as to whether "the Conservatives have learned from their past mistakes and are now more likely than Labour to deliver what they promise". In Hammersmith & Fulham there was net agreement of 1%. But others elsewhere disagreed (including voters in the two other Conservative-leaning constituencies) and the proposition was rejected in the twelve seats by a margin of 9%.

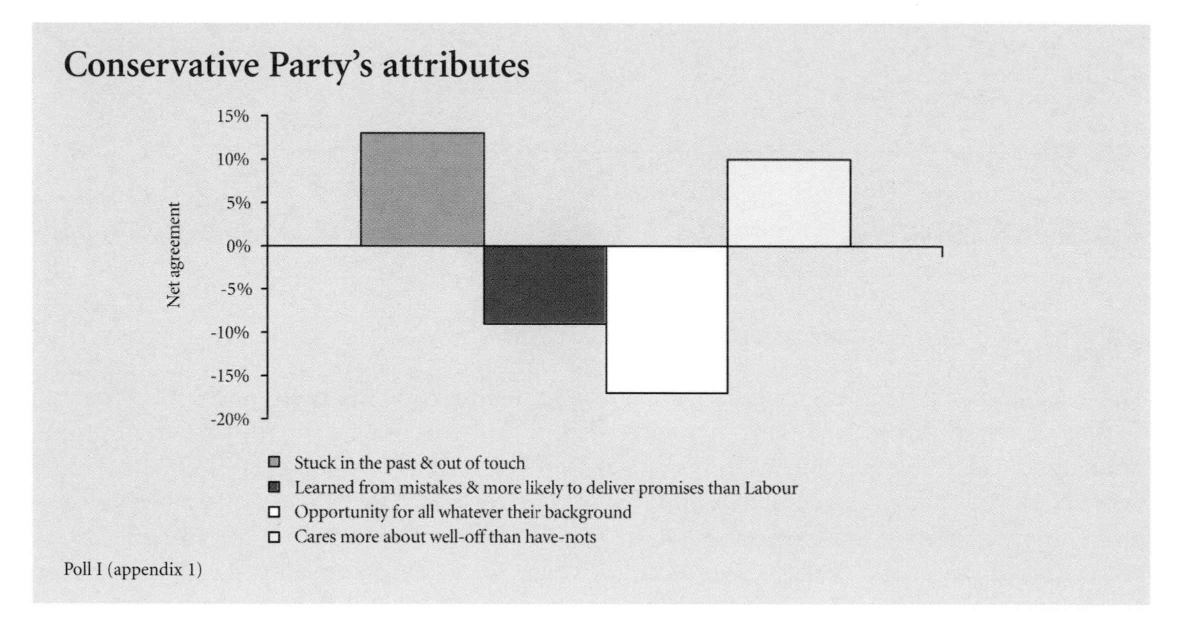

Poll I (appendix 1)

The notion that "the Conservative Party stands for opportunity for all and giving people, whatever their background, the best chance to get on in life", was decisively rejected in all twelve constituencies, with Conservative-leaning seats only slightly less likely to agree than the average margin of 17%. There was also clear agreement across the board that "the Conservative Party cares more about protecting the interests of well-off people than helping the have-nots" – although in this case there was a much clearer division between seats, with the margin of agreement in Labour-leaning constituencies twice that in those with a Tory lead.

The Labour Party emerged with a better reputation than the Conservatives and both leaders. By huge majorities, voters in all twelve constituencies agreed that "Labour has really changed from the past and won't go back to old Labour even when Tony Blair goes", and that "Labour used to be left-wing and is now in the centre or even on the right".

A clear majority across the seats felt that "Labour represents the interests of people from all different backgrounds", with even the Conservative-leaning seats recording margins in single figures.

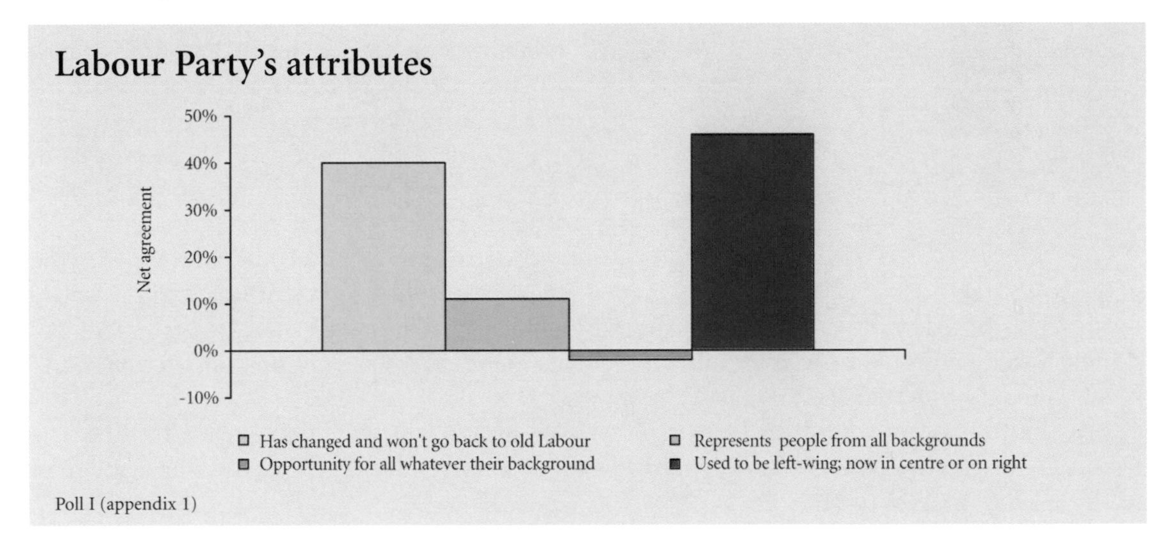

Poll I (appendix 1)

Much more closely contested was the suggestion that "Labour stands for opportunity for all: giving people, whatever their background, the best chance to get on in life". Here there was a much clearer divide between Labour-leaning seats, which all agreed, and Conservative-leaning seats, none of which did; one of the tied seats went each way. The resulting tiny margin of disagreement was in stark contrast to the 17% gap recorded for the Conservatives on the same measure.

A telling illustration of how voters regarded the two main parties was offered in The Times in March[44]. Summaries of the Conservative and Labour immigration policies[45] were read to respon-

44 Poll conducted by Populus 4-6 March, published in The Times 8-12 March 2005, sample 1,524.

45 Conservative: "They will set an annual limit on the number of immigrants able to enter Britain, and give priority to those who would make a positive contribution, as they do in Australia. They will change the work permit system so that people coming into Britain on a temporary permit are no longer able to settle here permanently. They will set up 24 hour surveillance at ports and airports, stop people who are not genuine refugees applying for asylum, and introduce health checks for immigrants to detect things like HIV, hepatitis and TB". Labour: "They will introduce a points system to ensure that those who enter Britain will benefit the country and end the right for immigrants to bring in their relatives. They will only allow skilled workers to settle long-term in the UK. They will introduce English language tests for those who want to stay permanently, and expand detention for failed asylum seekers".

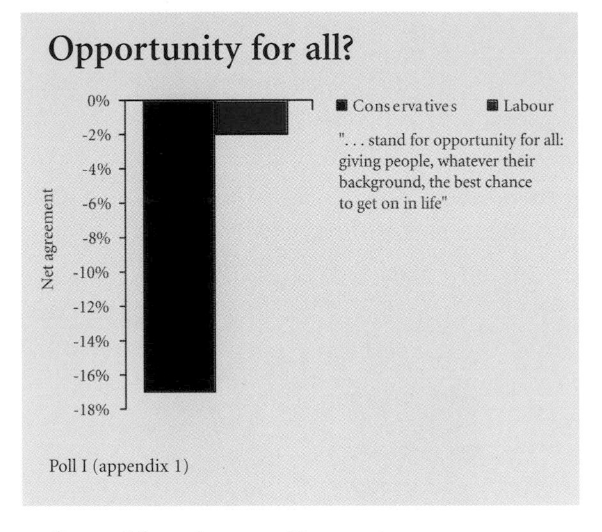

Poll I (appendix 1)

dents, who were asked whether or not they agreed with each. However, only half the respondents were told which policy was which; the others were told that each was a policy "that one of the political parties has proposed".

Approval of the Labour policy was similar whether respondents realised its provenance or not: net agreement was 34% when attributed, and 32% when not. Though approval for the Conservative policy was higher in both groups, the effect of attributing it to the Tories was dramatic.

Unattributed, 73% of voters agreed with the policy, with only 18% disagreeing: net agreement of 55%. But the group that was told the policy had been proposed by the Conservatives agreed by a much smaller margin of 43%. Agreement was slightly lower at 70%, but disagreement was 9 points higher at 27%, with those answering "don't know" down from 9% to 3%.

The effect on swing voters was clearer still. While only 17% of them disagreed with the unattributed Conservative policy, 29% disagreed when they knew who had proposed it. Net agreement fell by 16%, from 57% to 41%.

In other words, the Conservative label was undermining its ability to sell its policies. The drop in net agreement between the unattributed and attributed descriptions suggested that one voter in eight – and one in six swing voters - had such a negative view of the Conservative Party's brand that they would oppose a policy they actually agreed with rather than support a Tory proposal.

In Their own Words

In six of our twelve selected marginal seats I commissioned focus groups to examine in more depth how voters saw the campaign and the factors that were likely to determine their vote[46].

While polls say how many people have certain views, focus groups are a way of probing how people think about particular issues and why they hold the opinions they do. A group comprises eight or ten people who fit a certain specified profile - for this exercise, people who voted Labour in 2001 but were now undecided between Labour and the Conservatives. They took part in a

46 Gillingham, Hammersmith & Fulham, Kettering, Peterborough, The Wrekin and Wirral West. Research item J: see Appendix 1. All focus groups were observed and reported to me by a member of my own political team.

structured 90-minute discussion, led by a professional moderator, designed to explore their perceptions of the parties, their leaders, and local and national issues.

In all groups, most people were able to name their MP and apart from occasional minor gripes ("we never see him in Thrapston"), those who had an opinion usually regarded the local Member as hard-working and helpful. This appeared to have little bearing on people's voting intention though, with most participants saying that national issues and leaders would have much more influence on their decision. There was usually little awareness of the Conservative candidate, and in some places nobody in the groups knew his or her name – further underlining the advantage of incumbency.

The groups raised a wide range of concerns and only rarely did local issues feature prominently, such as in Kettering where participants complained about the rapid growth of new housing with no corresponding improvement in infrastructure or services.

Immigration was a recurring theme in the discussions, particularly in Peterborough, Kettering and Gillingham. Participants here thought that there were, in their respective areas, thousands of asylum seekers and illegal immigrants (between which the distinction was rather blurred) who were entitled to very generous benefits and responsible for a good deal of local crime. Anecdotes were frequently offered in support of these convictions.

"They've got all these scams they do," reported a woman in Gillingham, "where one pretends to fall down and everyone crowds round to help while others rob you". A man in the same town complained: "I was out of work for four weeks and I was given £56 a fortnight. Some Kosovan turns up next to me in line and gets £2,000 straight off".

Another man, also in Gillingham, told how his friend "went to the doctor's to get an appointment and was told to wait four days. A Kosovan turned up next to him to speak to the receptionist and got an appointment for 20 minutes' time. My friend was really annoyed and asked why, and was told it was a government thing, they have to give them an appointment".

"You see them in restaurants and bars," said a man in Peterborough, "and they get an allowance for their cars". "And their mobile phone," chipped in another. "And their leather jacket and a house".

The groups were often ready to blame the government for the situation and compared Britain's approach to immigration unfavourably with that of Australia. Several had also heard Michael Howard speaking on the subject and remarked that he had been prepared to talk sense on a controversial issue. However, their innate caution about election promises together with a feeling that the situation was beyond the control of politicians, or that the damage had been done, helped to prevent many even in these groups from deciding to vote Conservative on the basis of immigration alone.

Participants expressed dissatisfaction with Labour over a broad spectrum of issues, most often including law and order and the perceived inability or unwillingness of the police to deal with crime and anti-social behaviour ("the little blighters running around, and you can't touch them because of the human rights thing"); failure to improve public services fast enough, often because of excessive bureaucracy; the hospital 'superbug' MRSA; the war in Iraq; rising tax; pensions; or university tuition fees. These criticisms were often linked to a feeling that Labour had failed to live up to expectations: a regular complaint, voiced by a woman in The Wrekin, being: "I think back to what they promised when they first came in and it hasn't happened".

There was no corresponding feeling in the groups that a Conservative government would bring improvements in any or all of these areas. This was for a combination of reasons, including the distrust of politicians' promises expressed throughout the discussion ("they're all the same – they promise this, but will it happen?"), lack of confidence in Michael Howard, and the fact that few people were aware of any specific Conservative policy proposals - which is not surprising given the minuscule rates of recall for Tory messages or activities found in the daily tracker poll.

One issue on which the Conservatives had made an impression on some of the groups was their pledge to deal with the problem of illegal building developments by travellers. Some participants acknowledged that there was a problem with such developments in some areas, but the policy also caused puzzlement and a feeling that the party seemed to be picking on a mostly harmless minority, particularly since many understood the proposals to be rather more draconian than the Conservatives intended. A woman in Kettering, when asked what she recalled the Conservatives talking about recently, replied, "the gypsies – putting them in jail. I haven't got any on my field but it's a bit desperate".

Both leaders came in for a great deal of criticism from the groups. Tony Blair was seen by many as insincere, arrogant, trying to please everyone, dishonest, a puppet of President Bush and sometimes personally irritating ("it's so annoying the way he has to pause before he speaks").

Many of the participants disapproved of the war in Iraq, which they identified with Mr Blair personally. The main criticisms were that the prime minister had simply followed instructions from President Bush, leading some to conclude that he was weak, and that he had misled the nation about the presence of weapons of mass destruction. As the discussion on Mr Blair progressed, though, two notable things sometimes happened. First, it became clear that even those who had been angry about Iraq had few other strong objections to the prime minister himself. One woman in Hammersmith & Fulham said, "I wouldn't have much gripe with him if it wasn't for the war".

Secondly, as condemnation of Mr Blair over Iraq intensified, some of the women in particular found themselves leaping to his defence. "He did have the courage of his convictions," said a woman in Kettering. "There must have been intelligence. He couldn't go and find the weapons personally, so it was on his convictions and he was a strong leader". Another in Hammersmith & Fulham, feeling that the prime minister had been in a difficult position, said after very bitter criticism of him by the group, "I can't help but be sympathetic towards him". "I would be too," confessed her neighbour. "He's trying".

Men were much more determinedly negative about Mr Blair. As with the women, though, despite a barrage of criticism over what they saw as a failure to stand up to the Americans or his attempts to please everybody ("wet – just seems to fold on everything"), some of the men confessed that they couldn't bring themselves to dislike him. "Blair is a likeable bloke," observed a man in Peterborough. "You find yourself wanting to believe him".

Despite the long list of criticisms of Mr Blair, most groups had a more positive view of him than of Michael Howard. While Mr Howard was more effective than his recent predecessors and gained some credit for straight talking on controversial issues ("he will stand up for what he thinks"), in comparison with the prime minister he was widely seen as insubstantial and lacking authority. A man in Peterborough noted, "When Blair was first in he was dynamic. You thought 'he's leading that party'. But you look at Howard and think 'Nah'. You wouldn't want to be at the UN and think 'there goes our leader'."

The discussions accorded with the findings of our polls in the twelve seats that more people agreed with Mr Howard on important issues than felt he had the necessary qualities to be prime minister. The Conservative leader was also dogged by Ann Widdecombe's notorious observation that Mr Howard had "something of the night" about him (by which she meant, according to a Peterborough participant, that he was "a shifty bastard").

When discussing the parties themselves, groups could not identify any real differences of principle to separate Labour from the Conservatives – a point which led a woman in Kettering to say that even if they found out over the course of the campaign what each party's policies were, "you couldn't distinguish which was which". As a man in Peterborough observed: "years ago you could separate them, but not any more. It's whoever offers the best guarantees and stands up for what they say".

When it came to making this decision, though, many participants were frustrated or even exasperated. They complained about the overabundance of negative campaigning and what they felt was the difficulty in establishing exactly what each party stood for and what it planned to do. A woman in The Wrekin declared: "I would like someone to come to the door and say the nitty gritty, what they will do for me. I could sit in front of the internet but I don't have the time".

Several found themselves in the position of wanting to vote against the government, but without removing Labour from office. A man in Gillingham concluded: "I think I'll vote Tory, not because I want the Tories to win but because I want Labour to win by a smaller majority, giving a clear message". But another in Kettering was still wavering: "If I'd voted Conservative [and they won] I'd think, 'what the hell have I done?' "

Several participants around the country resolved to pay close attention to the campaigns in search of a positive reason to vote, but usually more in hope than expectation. "I'm trying to take it in," a man in The Wrekin said. "I'm disgruntled but there is nothing to make me feel that voting on 5th May will make my life better on 6th May".

Keep on Tracking

Meanwhile, our daily tracker poll[47] continued to monitor the ups and downs of the near-term campaign. Throughout March and until the very beginning of the general election campaign itself, Labour maintained their steady lead over the Conservatives.

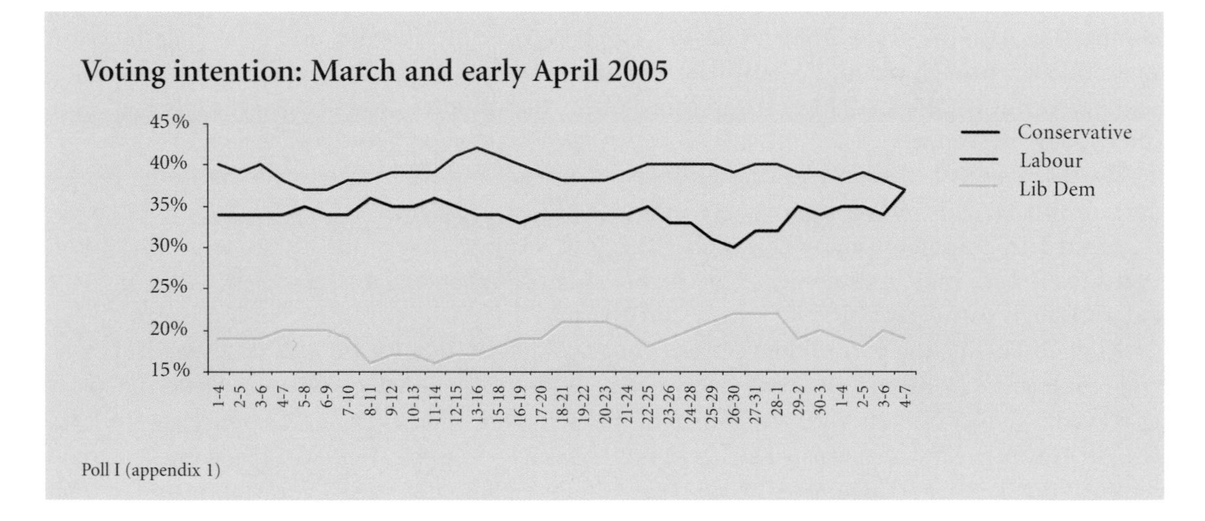

Labour's lead narrowed slightly in the wake of the Liberal Democrats' Spring Conference over the first weekend in March, at which Charles Kennedy launched his party's election slogan, "the real alternative". While Labour support recovered steadily, returning to levels in the high 30s, the Conservatives stayed at around 34% for most of March. It fell to 30% over the Easter weekend and recovered to end the pre-campaign period tied with Labour on 37%.

47 Poll F: see Appendix 1.

Recall of Conservative activities and messages between the beginning of March and the announcement of the general election was even lower than had been the case in January and February. During this time nine issues were recalled by 2% or more of voters over at least one four-day period. Meanwhile, key campaign messages including promises of more police, better value for money, higher spending on public services, restoring school discipline, tougher sentences for criminals and more choice of schools were each mentioned by 1% of voters or fewer. Each day, between 73% and 83% of voters said they could remember hearing nothing at all about the Conservatives.

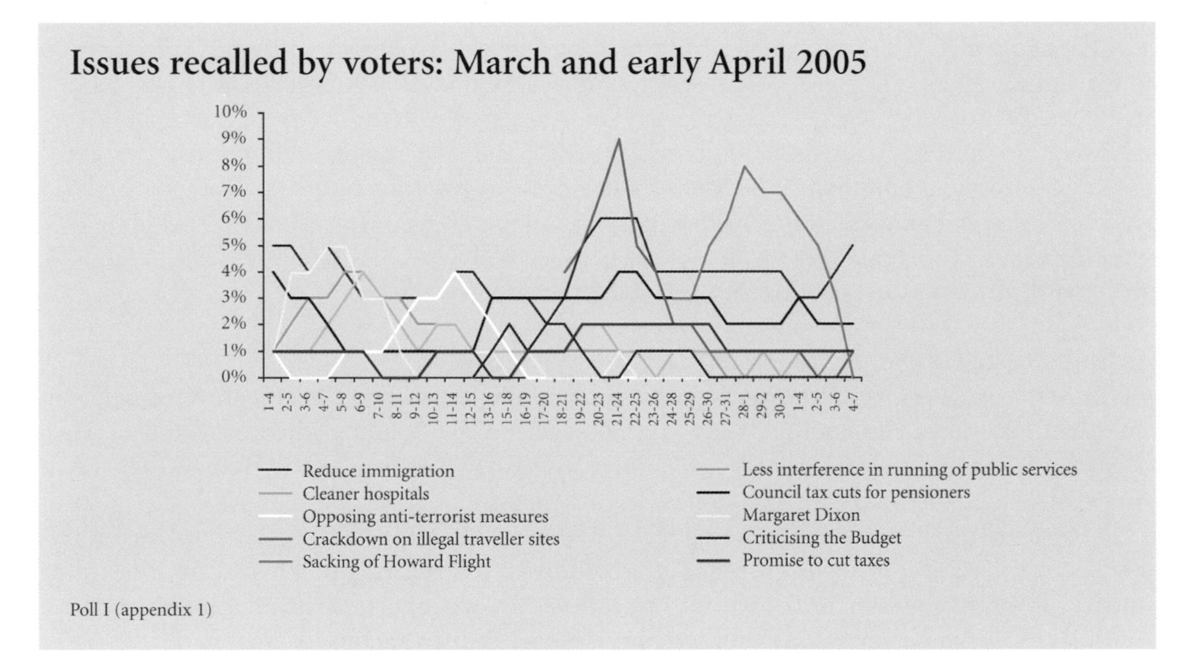

Issues recalled by voters: March and early April 2005

Poll I (appendix 1)

During this period only four activities or messages were ever recalled by 5% or more voters when asked what they had recently noticed the Conservatives saying or doing: immigration, the case of Margaret Dixon, the proposed crackdown on illegal building developments by travellers, and the sacking and subsequent deselection of Howard Flight.

For immigration, this rate of recall represents a levelling off since the start of the year, when it had peaked at 31% on 24-27 January. The Conservatives maintained a comfortable lead over Labour on the subject of between 10% and 22%.

Mrs Dixon's shoulder

At prime minister's questions on 2 March, Michael Howard raised the case of Margaret Dixon, a pensioner from Warrington whose shoulder operation he claimed had been cancelled seven times. The case caused a furious political row that dominated the news for several days, culminating in an unscheduled visit to Warrington General Hospital by the Health Secretary, John Reid, but appeared to bring little benefit to the Conservatives. Although recall of the issue peaked at a relatively high 5%, it had fallen to zero within a week. The highest level of recall coincided with a Labour lead of 12% on "improving public services", roughly the level recorded throughout the second half of February. By the end of the month Labour's lead on public services had doubled.

A Populus poll for The Times in March[48] helps to explain why the episode apparently failed to work to the Conservatives' advantage. Voters were split down the middle as to whether Mrs Dixon's case represented a broader problem in the health service: 44% agreed with the statement "cases like this are now very rare in the NHS, which is improving overall", and 44% disagreed. But nearly two thirds (64%) rejected the proposition "if the Conservatives were in government their policies for the NHS would bring an end to cases like this", with only 22% in support. An even greater 72% - including 77% of swing voters - concurred that "politicians are being cynical when they raise issues like this and do so for party advantage, not because they care about the person's suffering".

Travellers and human rights

On 21 March Michael Howard made a speech condemning the fact that "if you are a traveller you can use the so-called Human Rights Act to bend planning law, building wherever you like". This, he said, was "one of the reasons why the Conservative Party is reviewing the Human Rights Act. And if it can't be improved, we'll scrap it".[49]

The statement achieved unusually high recall, peaking at 9% and reflecting the spontaneous references to the subject in focus groups. But according to the tracking poll it had no discernible impact on voting intention or the parties' respective leads on important issues. It may be notable – although it is not possible to say with certainty whether the two are linked – that in the days after Mr Howard's statement the proportion of C2 and DE voters saying the Conservative Party shared their values rose, while the proportion of ABC1 saying the same remained static.

One Flight down

Howard Flight, the Conservative Party's deputy chairman and former shadow chief secretary to the Treasury, was sacked from the front bench on 25 March and subsequently deselected as a par-

48 4-6 March 2005, sample 1,524, published in The Times 8-12 March 2005.

49 Press release, 21 March 2005.

liamentary candidate in his constituency of Arundel & South Downs after giving the impression, in a secretly recorded speech, that the Conservatives' intentions to limit public expenditure went beyond those set out in the James Review. The episode was a blow to the Tories, who had gone to great lengths to establish the credibility of their tax and spending plans and defend their claim to be able to invest more in front-line public services while cutting taxes by £4 billion. Days before the incident Labour had been on the defensive over their assertion that the Conservatives planned to cut public spending rather than, as the Conservatives maintained, to increase it more slowly than Labour planned to do.

In the week following Mr Flight's sacking there were increases in the Labour lead on improving public services, managing the economy and tax, and dips in net agreement on all attributes for the Conservatives. Tory voting intention also fell, with the Liberal Democrats, whose share had been rising since the launch of their '10 promises' advertising campaign on 22 March, the main beneficiaries.

Despite his uncompromising decision to sack Mr Flight both as a party officer and as a candidate, a poll[50] the following weekend found that Mr Howard was regarded as the weakest of the three main party leaders. 42% of voters regarded him as "strong", compared to 66% for Mr Blair and 45% for Mr Kennedy, while 38% saw him as "weak" – the highest such rating of the three. Only 37% (and only 30% of swing voters) thought he had good judgment in a crisis, compared to 38% for Mr Blair and 44% for Mr Kennedy. Nearly two thirds (62%) thought that rather than being honest about what he would do, Mr Howard had a secret policy agenda. (This was thought to be even more true of Mr Blair, with 73% thinking he hid unpopular policies).

Discussion of the subject in our focus groups also suggested that Mr Howard's actions had done little to boost his reputation among voters. Most participants recognised that Mr Flight's remarks were potentially damaging to the Conservatives and that Mr Howard wanted to be seen as a strong leader. While a few thought he had done the right thing, most people thought the Tory leader's actions had been disproportionate and, therefore, more damaging than Mr Flight's speech.

In particular, they felt that expelling Mr Flight from the party had demonstrated panic and lack of judgment and highlighted a story which would otherwise probably not have reached them: "It's drawn more attention to it," said a woman in Hammersmith & Fulham. None of us would have been aware of it. It would have been a little bit on the second page". "Over the top. Shows he lacks political judgment. It's like scoring an own goal". "It's panicking. It shows weakness, actually". "We all know that politicians play with figures, so to sack someone because he says they might cut a bit more…it sounds like a non-issue".

50 Conducted by Populus 1-3 April 2005, sample 1,513, published in The Times 5-7 April 2005.

At least two other notable political events took place during this period of the near-term campaign. On 11 March, the Prevention of Terrorism Act was passed after a marathon sitting in the House of Commons. The Conservatives had joined forces with Labour rebels to oppose the legislation, disagreeing with the government over the circumstances in which suspected terrorists could be subject to control orders, including house arrest, without trial, and demanding a 'sunset clause' under which the Act would automatically expire after a defined period. A relatively high 4% of voters recalled the Conservatives' opposition to the law, and over the following days Labour's poll lead began to climb steadily. On 11-15 March the Conservatives fell eight points behind Labour on the issue of dealing properly with crime, matching their lowest rating on the subject since the beginning of the year. In the days after the Act was passed there were also sharp drops in the proportions saying the party "would do a good job in government" and "shares my values", and a more gentle dip in the proportion saying the Conservatives "have plans to deal with the important problems". (A separate poll of the 130 Labour marginals a few weeks later[51] found that while in these seats the Conservatives were the most trusted party on crime, by 53% to 47%, Labour had a 51%-49% edge on security and terrorism).

Gordon Brown's Budget on 16 March featured a £200 council tax rebate for pensioners aged over 65, a higher threshold for stamp duty on house purchases, and an increase in child tax credit. In the days immediately following the Conservatives narrowed Labour's lead on spending taxpayers' money well and the amount of tax ordinary people pay, but within a week they

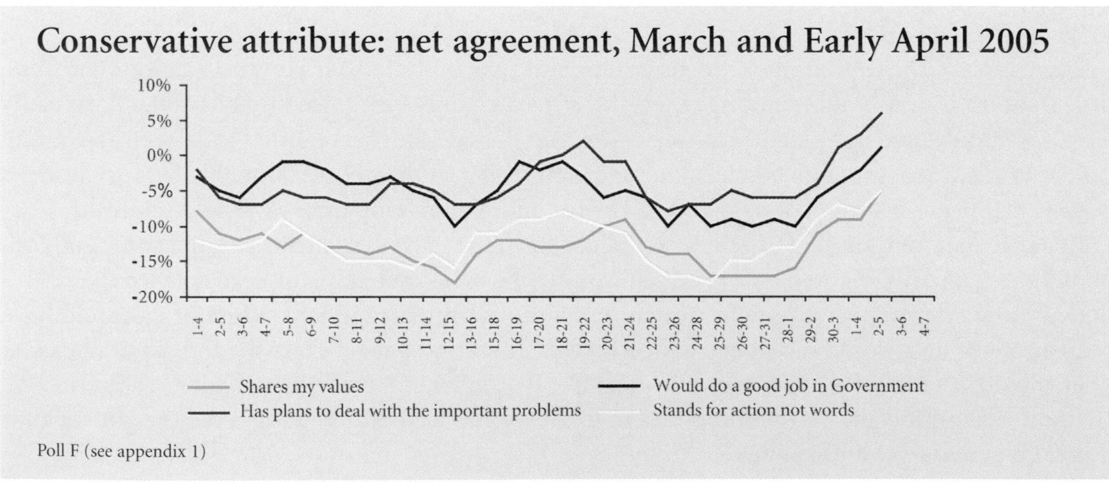

Poll F (see appendix 1)

51 Poll G: see Appendix 1.

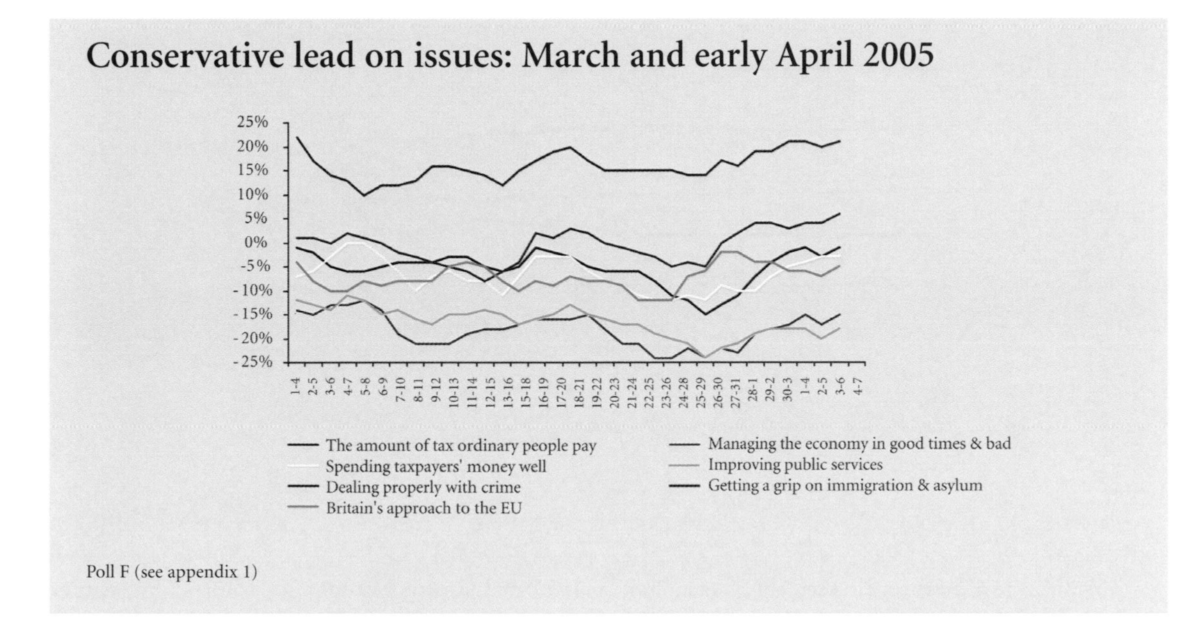

Conservative lead on issues: March and early April 2005

Poll F (see appendix 1)

had lost ground. By the end of the month Labour had extended their lead on managing the economy to 24%.

In their poll for The Times in early March[52], Populus asked what voters had made of the pre-election campaign. The answers revealed a desire on the part of voters to get to the bottom of the issues and make an informed choice, but confusion about policies and frustration with the antics of the parties. More than half (55%) claimed to "take an active interest in what the political parties say in their campaigns", but only just over a third (35%) said they had "a clearer idea of the policies of the main political parties than I did a few weeks ago", with 61% disagreeing. 58% thought "there doesn't seem much difference between the parties any more", and an overwhelming 80% agreed that "the parties have mainly just been attacking each other rather than explaining their policies".

The following month only 22% of voters said they were satisfied with the Labour government overall, a further 33% said they were dissatisfied with Labour but still preferred them to the Tories. Less than a third of voters (32%) said they would prefer a Conservative government – a proportion that had steadily declined since the question was first asked in February 2004[53].

52 4-6 March 2005, sample 1,524, published in The Times 8-12 March 2005.

53 Populus polls for The Times conducted 6-8 February, 7-9 May, 2-5 September 2004, and 5-7 March and 1-3 April 2005.

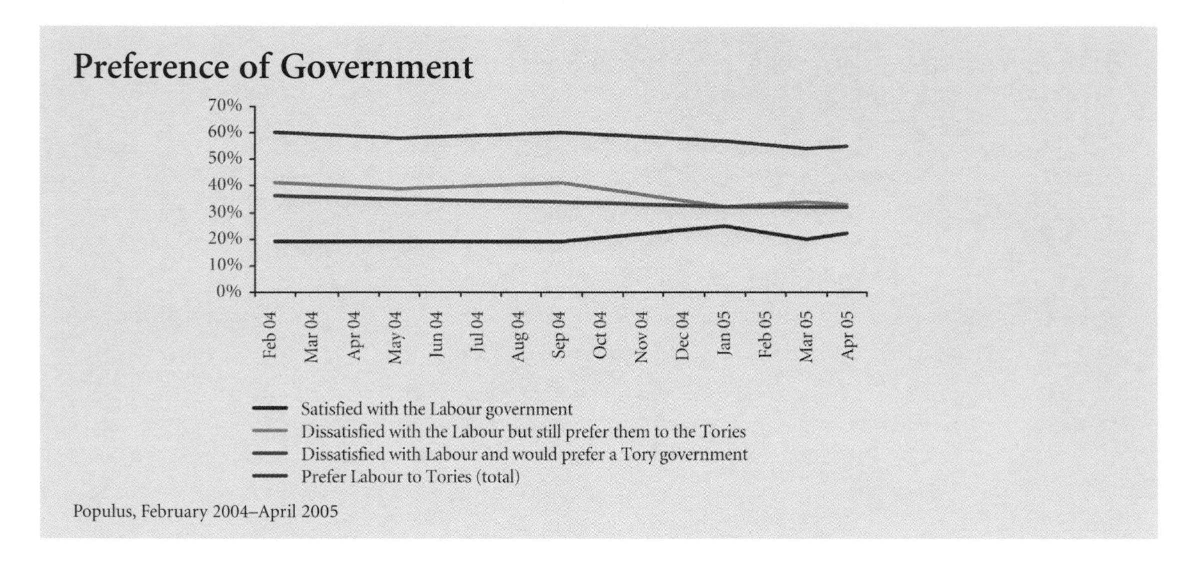

Preference of Government

Populus, February 2004–April 2005

In their final poll before the election was called, ICM[54] put Labour 3 points ahead on 37%. Voters preferred Tony Blair as prime minister to Michael Howard by 38% to 26%.

54 Conducted 1-3 April 2005, published in The Guardian 5 April 2005, sample 1,507.

Chapter Four

The General Election Campaign

On the morning of Tuesday 5 April 2005 Tony Blair stood in Downing Street and confirmed (the Queen having graciously consented to dissolve parliament) that a general election would be held on 5 May. Speaking without a podium and without notes, the prime minister described Labour's "driving mission for a third term", entrenching economic stability and improvements in public services. His mission would be driven by values; he wanted a country where success was determined by "hard work and merit, not privilege or background" and where "people who play by the rules get on". It was, he said, "a big choice, a big decision. The British people are the boss and they are the ones that will make it".

Launching his own campaign later that day Michael Howard said the choice at hand was clear. People could "reward Mr Blair for eight years of broken promises and vote for another five years of talk, or they can vote Conservative". While the Labour government had "lost the plot", Mr Howard's party had taken a stand and were committed to action on the issues that matter to hard-working Britons. The Conservatives were offering a better way (conspicuously similar to that described by Mr Blair) in which "people who do the right thing, who play by the rules" were rewarded. Mr Howard expanded on the ten words that described the five promises launched at the Conservative conference six months earlier and invited voters to hold him to account by sticking the party's Timetable for Action – its plan for the first month of a Conservative government - to their fridge door. Insisting that Britain could not be made a better place if difficult issues were swept under the carpet, he pledged not to be distracted by "the smirking politics of Mr Blair" or "the woolly thinking of the Liberal Democrats". Mr Blair, he said, was already "secretly grinning" about the prospect of his third election victory, but people didn't have to settle for that: "If you're thinking what we're thinking, it's time for urgent action on the things that really matter".

The two speeches, as reported by ITV News, were scrutinised by undecided voters in our focus groups[55] in The Wrekin. For these voters, the two performances encapsulated the leaders' respective flaws. Mr Blair was thought to look nervous, highlighting concerns about his honesty. "His demeanour and body language don't go with what comes out of his mouth," said one participant. "You can't trust him even if you want to". Another thought that for a speech setting out the case for a third Labour term it was rather short on specifics: "Given he was the one person who knew he was going to make a speech he didn't seem very well prepared. Hopes, dreams, aspirations, but nothing very concrete. Not 'we've done this in the past and this is what we'll do now'."

Mr Howard's performance was even less well received. The groups felt that he lacked authority and that the balance of his remarks was very negative – for them, a sign that he had little of substance to offer. "He doesn't strike me as being leadership material," said one man, and one of the women was more forthright: "Grey, old, smarmy and creepy". "At least Tony Blair talked about values," observed another. "Michael Howard just slagged off Labour".

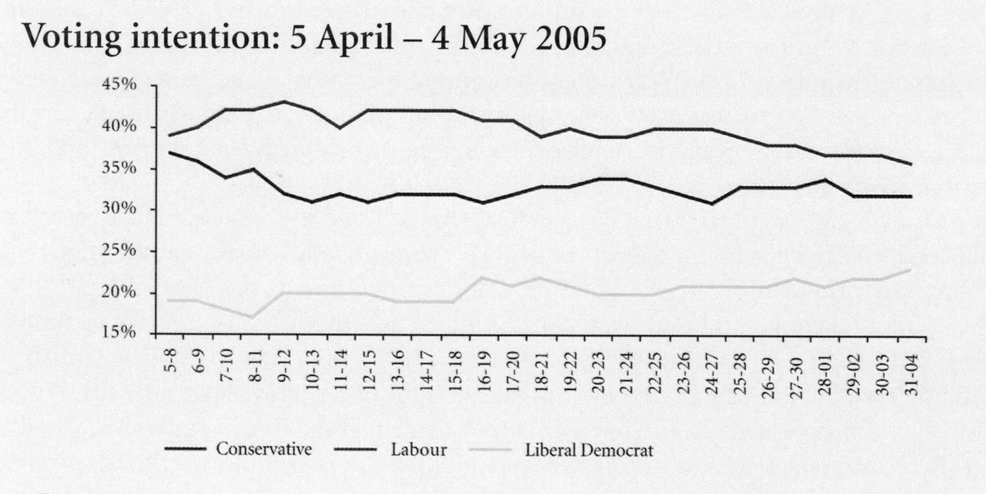

Poll F (see appendix 1)

According to our daily tracking poll[56], there was little dramatic movement in voting intention between the formal start of the campaign and 4 May, although clear trends were evident. Labour support quickly climbed above 40%, where it remained for most of April, before declining to the

55 The only one of the twelve sets of focus groups in marginal seats to be conducted after the election had been called. Research item J: see Appendix 1.

56 Poll F: see Appendix 1.

36% recorded the day before the election. From 37% at the time of the election announcement, Conservative support fell into the low 30s, levelling off at 32% from the beginning of May. Only the Liberal Democrats saw a net increase in support over the course of the formal election campaign, from below 20% in early April to 23% a month later.

There was similarly little change in voters' confidence in the two parties on important issues. The Conservatives maintained a comfortable lead over Labour on immigration of between 11 and 24 points throughout the campaign. The advantage on crime changed hands four times between 5 April and polling day, with the Conservatives finishing 5 points ahead.

Despite the Tories' ubiquitous campaign theme of lower taxes and better value for money, Labour held a steady lead on the amount of tax ordinary people pay and spending taxpayers' money well.

However, this was not because voters thought Labour would not increase taxes. In a poll for The Times in December 2004[57], Populus found that 71% of voters expected taxes to rise if Labour were re-elected. While only 48% expected higher taxes under a Conservative government, this still dwarfed the sum of the 13% who believed that taxes would fall under the Tories and the 26% who expected the level of taxes to remain the same.

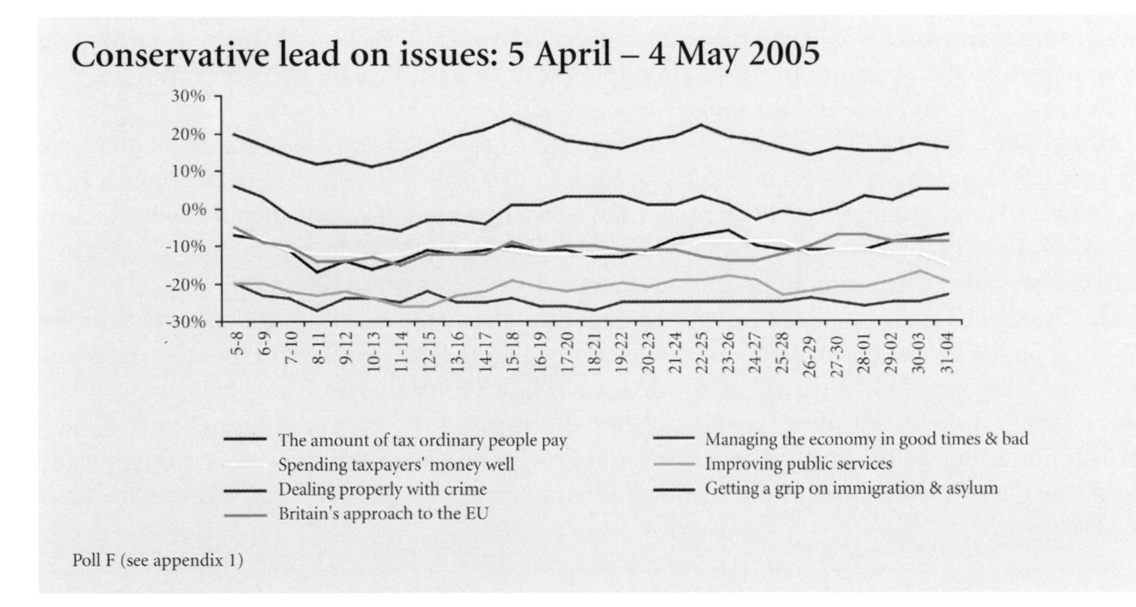

Poll F (see appendix 1)

57 Conducted 3-5 December 2004, published in The Times 6-8 December 2004.

On the broader question of managing the economy in good times and bad, Labour consistently led by a greater margin than that held by the Conservatives on immigration. Despite going to some lengths to try to establish their credibility on the issue, including the James Review process, seeking authentication of their budgetary arithmetic by the Institute for Fiscal Studies, and enduring criticism from some commentators on their own side for the caution of their tax cutting plans, the Conservatives never made a real dent in this lead in the run-up to the election.

However, given the state of public opinion on the issue over the preceding months and years it would have been rather surprising if they had. According to MORI[58], Labour had held an unbroken lead on managing the economy since May 1998, rising to 30 points by April 2005. Conservative efforts to convince voters that their economic policies were more credible than Labour's (beginning in the 1997 parliament with the prophecy that Britain was heading for a "downturn made in Downing Street", followed by numerous warnings of black holes, stealth taxes and pensions timebombs) came up against an apparently insurmountable obstacle: people thought the economy was on the right track, benefiting them personally.

In six polls for the Daily Telegraph during the general election campaign YouGov consistently found that well over half of voters expected the financial situation of their household to get better or stay the same over the following 12 months. Their final poll before the election found 23% thought their situation would improve, 34% expected it to stay the same (which, given general acceptance that the economy was performing well, can be regarded on the whole as a positive answer) and 37% said it would get worse.[59]

In a Populus poll for The Times[60] conducted a few days before the election, 77% of voters thought the economy would perform well for the country over the next year, net optimism having improved among supporters of all parties since the beginning of April, when the question was last asked. Exactly three quarters thought the economy would do well "for me and my family". Even Conservative voters could not bring themselves to disagree on either score.

The Times December poll also sought to establish whom the voters credited or, as the case may be, blamed for the performance of the economy. The 64% of people who thought the economy was doing well were precisely evenly divided as to whether this was "largely because of" or "not much to do with" Gordon Brown's policies. But most of the 27% who thought the economy was not doing well thought that this was not much to do with the chancellor either, meaning only 11% of voters thought the economy was performing badly and that this was the fault of Mr Brown.

58 MORI Political Trends: Best Party on Key Issues. See mori.com

59 3-4 May 2005, published in the Daily Telegraph 5 May 2005, sample 3,962. Also 5-6, 12-14, 19-21, 22-24 and 26-28 April. See yougov.co.uk.

60 Conducted 28-29 April 2005, published in The Times 1 May 2005, sample 716.

Vote Brown, Get Blair, "Oh Good"

During the campaign the chancellor frequently appeared side-by-side with the prime minister, a fact which fascinated the reporters and commentators who had analysed every nuance of the pair's relationship since Mr Blair assumed the Labour leadership in 1994. On the first full day of campaigning the prime minister told a press conference that Mr Brown, who was sitting next to him, was the best chancellor Britain had had for 100 years, adding that "it would be pretty foolish to put that at risk" - a phrase which was taken as a guarantee that that he would remain at the Treasury if Labour won.

The campaign double-act suggests that Labour strategists had heeded poll findings, no doubt supplemented by private research, that the chancellor was a significant asset to Labour in terms of public opinion.

Earlier in the year, ICM[61] had found that while nearly as many voters thought Tony Blair was an electoral liability to Labour (43%) as thought he was an asset (45%), they considered Gordon Brown an asset by a margin of 41% (63%-22%).

The following month, soon after the Budget, YouGov[62] found that more than half of voters (52%) thought Mr Brown was doing a better job as chancellor than Mr Blair was doing as prime minister, with only 17% saying the opposite. Of the two, 40% would rather see Mr Brown in Number 10, compared to only 30% who would prefer Mr Blair.

In a mid-campaign poll for The Times[63], though, Populus found that voters were not convinced that the pair's display of togetherness signified any lessening of the supposed antagonism between them. Nearly two thirds (65%) thought the prime minister and chancellor had "significantly different views on many key issues", and 67% agreed that the two "want voters to think they like and respect each other, but once the election is over they will become rivals again".

Findings like these, together with voters' satisfaction and optimism on the economy, help to explain why the Conservatives abandoned their proposed campaign slogan of "vote Blair, get Brown", floated in the spring of 2004 and still being discussed by some at the autumn party conference.

As early as May 2004, ICM found that if Mr Brown took over as leader, Labour's poll lead would rise from 4 to 8 points, as undecided former Labour voters returned to the fold[64]. NOP found a similar situation in a poll for The Independent four months before the election[65], with the proportion of voters saying they would definitely support Labour rising from 23% to 31% if Mr Brown were leader, compared to only 18% for the Conservatives.

61 Poll conducted 18-20 February 2005, published in The Guardian 22 February 2005, sample 1003
62 Poll conducted 16-17 March 2005, published in the Daily Telegraph 21 March 2005, sample 1,303.
63 Conducted 21-23 April 2005, published in The Times 25 April 2005, sample 709.
64 Conducted 20-23 May 2004, published in The Guardian 26 May 2004, sample 1,002.
65 Conducted 7-9 January 2005, published in The Independent 11 January 2005, sample 951.

Mr Brown's popularity was underlined in our focus groups. Most participants, undecided voters who had supported Labour in 2001, did not know very much about him, but their general impression was of a solid, hard-working politician with an impressive record. "A bit rumpled but a good man", was the verdict of a woman in Hammersmith & Fulham, with another adding "he's the best thing about this government". Few were alarmed by the prospect of Mr Brown becoming prime minister. Indeed, the slogan "vote Blair, get Brown" nearly always worked in Labour's favour: "That," said a woman in Hammersmith & Fulham, "would swing it for me".

Unlike the prime minister, Michael Howard was unable to draw on the support of a high-profile, well-regarded colleague. During focus groups in The Wrekin[66], participants were shown a Conservative Party election broadcast, entitled 'Values', in which Mr Howard talked about his background and the Conservatives' pledges, and members of the shadow cabinet extolled their leader's virtues.

Although they thought the film was well-produced most people said the content was not enough to convince them to vote Tory, partly because of what they felt was a lack of detailed policy plans and partly because they did not take to Mr Howard. But perhaps the most striking element of their reaction was that most had assumed on first viewing that the clips of shadow cabinet ministers (whose appearance on screen was not accompanied by captions giving their name) were in fact 'vox pops' of ordinary voters or party supporters. Though mostly inoffensive and sometimes likeable, the featured politicians were "from the same mould" and none was thought to be very inspiring. "Some would be parliamentary workers in the office. That's presumably what that one was. A true blue Tory". "When I saw this last week I thought they were just Joe Public. I had no idea. It's quite a worry, that". One man summed up his view with an eloquent mix of metaphors: "They're a one-horse pony".

Public Services: All Delivery and No Spin?

As well as economic management, Labour maintained a robust advantage on improving public services, beginning and ending the formal campaign 20 points ahead of the Conservatives on the issue in the daily tracker. Public services have long been considered "Labour issues" (MORI have found clear Labour leads on education since March 1990, and on health since they first asked the question in 1978[67]). But although they identified and placed on the front page of their manifesto two totemic issues about which the public were concerned – MRSA in hospitals and poor discipline in schools – the Conservatives faced the same problem as they did with the economy: voters thought public services were improving.

66 26 April 2005. Research item J: see Appendix 1.

67 MORI Political Trends: Best Party On Key Issues. See mori.com

In March 2005[68], 73% of voters said that their experience of the NHS was good, up 7% since March 2004. 60% said their experience of schools was good, up 1%, and although only 49% said they had had generally good experience of transport, this proportion was up 8% on a year earlier. (For these questions, the poll sample was split: while half were asked about their own experience of public services, the other half were asked how well they thought such services were delivered nationally. In all cases, voters' experience of public services was better than their perception of them; also in all cases, this gap between experience and perception was narrowing).

Experience versus perception of public services: March 2005

Change since March 2004 in brackets

	Good	Bad	NET	Perception gap
The NHS - experience	73% (+7%)	23% (+3%)	50% (+4%)	5% (-15%)
The NHS - perception	64% (+8%)	19% (-11%)	45% (+19%)	
Schools - experience	60% (+1%)	21% (+8%)	39% (-7%)	10 % (-7%)
Schools - perception	52% (-3%)	23% (-3%)	29% (-)	
Transport - experience	49% (+8%)	43% (+2%)	6% (+6%)	11% (-9%)
Transport - perception	38% (+6%)	43% (-9%)	-5% (-15%)	

Populus

The Tory Campaign: Counterproductive or Just Ineffective?

Shifts in voters' perceptions of the Conservative Party's attributes during the campaign were more marked than in parties' leads on issues, or voting intention. However, the daily tracker found that despite ups and downs on all measures, there was a net fall in each one between the announcement of the election and polling day.

In other words, by the end of the Conservatives' general election campaign voters were less likely to think the party shared their values, less likely to think it had plans to deal with the important

68 Populus poll for The Times, conducted 4-6 March 2005, published 8-12 March 2005, sample 1,524. MORI Political Trends: Best Party On Key Issues. See mori.com

problems, less likely to think it would do a good job in government and less likely to think it stood for action not words than they had been at the beginning.

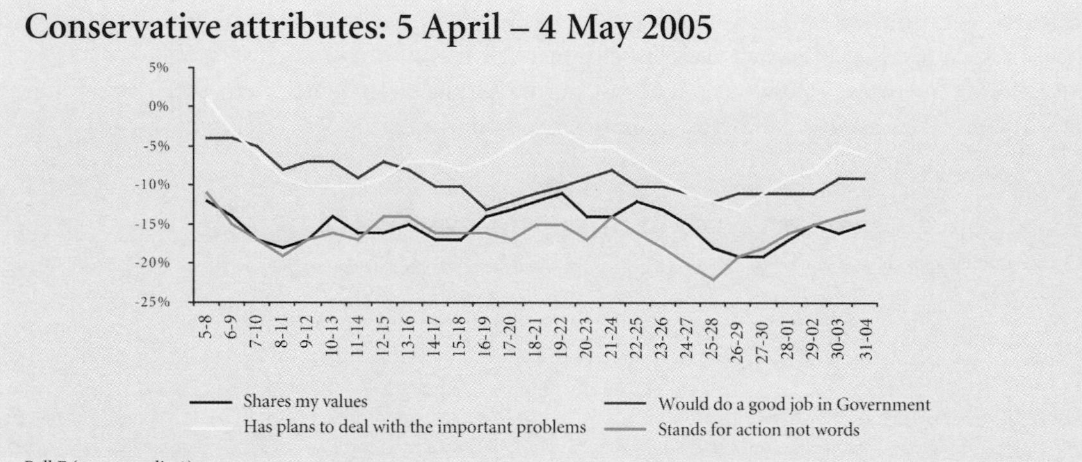

Poll F (see appendix 1)

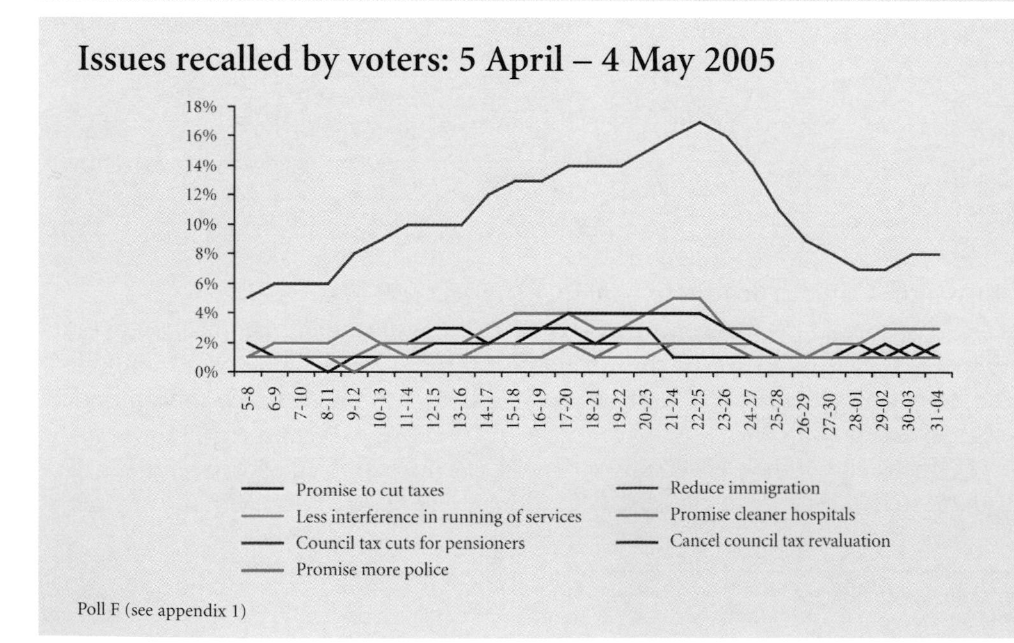

Poll F (see appendix 1)

As had been the case since the start of the year, immigration dominated voters' recall of Conservative messages and activities during the general election campaign. The promise of cleaner hospitals was the only other theme to have been recalled by 5% of people when asked what they could remember the Conservatives saying or doing in the previous few days. The proportion saying they could recall nothing at all dipped from 82% at the start of the formal campaign to 69% in the middle, but climbed back to 75% by the eve of poll, possibly reflecting people making up their minds and paying no further attention to the campaigns.

The Importance of Being Salient

As at the beginning of the year, the daily tracker showed little discernable relationship between recall of the Conservatives' immigration message and intention to vote for the party, or the proportions of voters feeling that the Tories had particular attributes.

An ICM poll for the Sunday Telegraph[69] midway through the campaign shed further light on the relationship between immigration and Conservative support. Though the party's lead on the issue was by this stage well established, 59% of all voters (and 60% of 'don't knows') said its policy of imposing annual limits to asylum and immigration made "no real difference" to how they intended to vote at the general election. While 24% said the policy made them more likely to vote

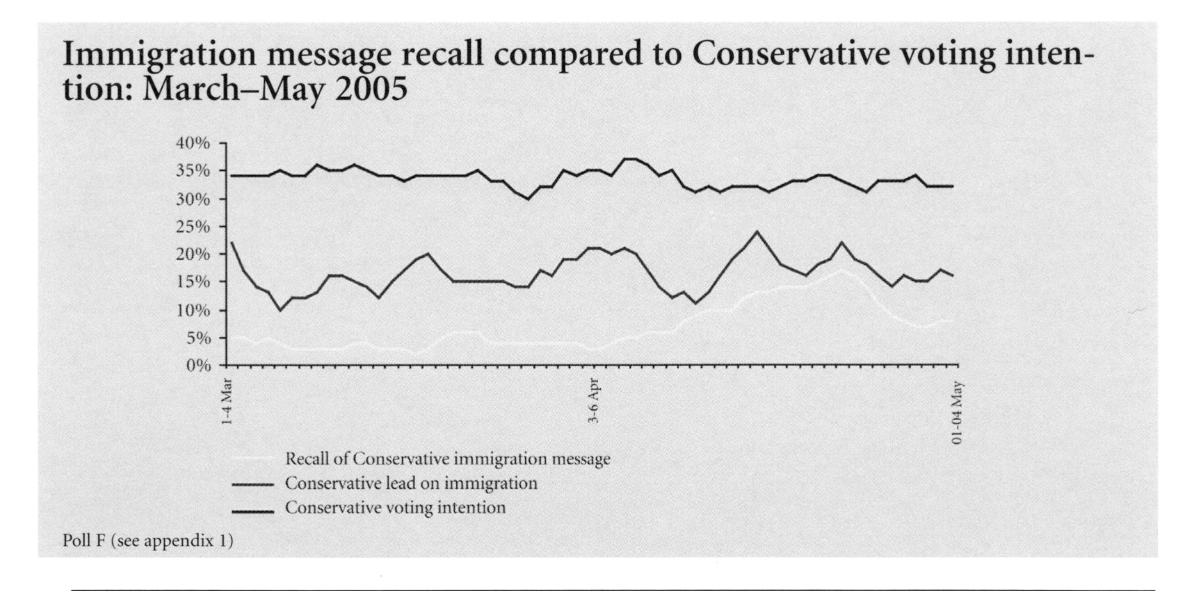

Immigration message recall compared to Conservative voting intention: March–May 2005

Poll F (see appendix 1)

69 Conducted 13-15 April 2005, published in the Sunday Telegraph 17 April 2005, sample 1,521.

Immigration message recall cf. Conservative attributes: March–May 2005

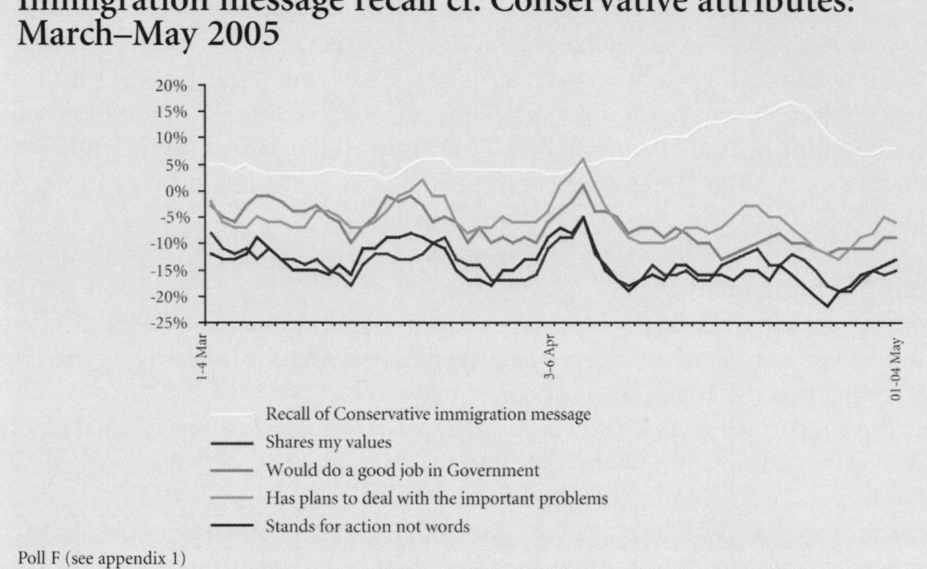

Poll F (see appendix 1)

Key issues, salience and party lead: 1st May– 3rd 2005

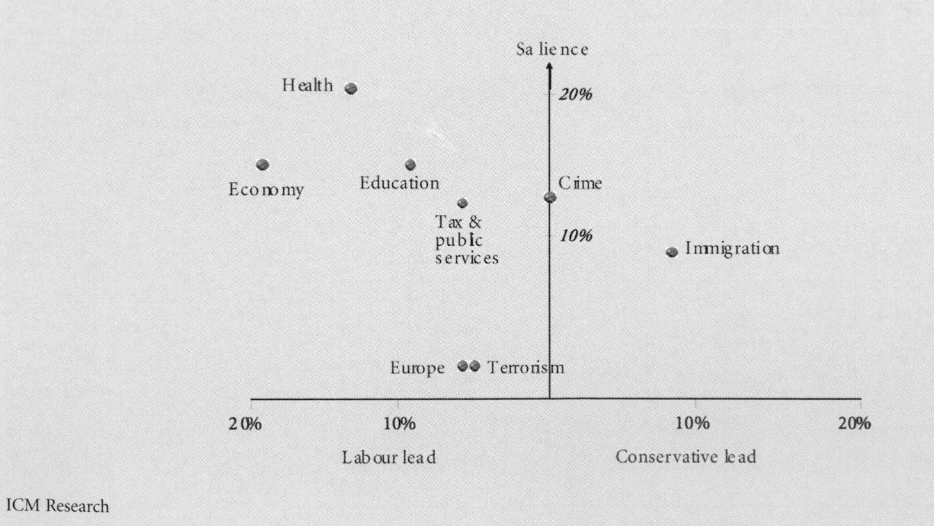

ICM Research

Conservative, this rose to 55% among Conservative voters. Indeed, nearly half of all those saying that the policy made them more likely to vote Tory had already stated their intention to do so – suggesting that the position on immigration had more success in reinforcing existing Conservative support than in drawing undecided voters to the party.

Throughout the campaign ICM tracked the salience and party advantage on a range of issues. Asked which of a range of issues "will be most important to you in your decision on how to vote in the next general election" and then, "irrespective of how you yourself will vote at the next election, which political party do you think is putting forward the best policies" on each, voters consistently gave Labour a clear lead on most of the issues most likely to influence their decision.

The final ICM poll before the election[70] gave Labour a clear lead of 13% over the Conservatives on health, which 21% of voters said was the most important issue in their voting decision. On education and the economy – the joint second most salient issues, each named by 15% of voters – Labour were ahead by 9% and 19% respectively. The only issue on which the Conservatives had a clear advantage was immigration – the most important issue in the minds of only 9% of voters (an increase of only 1% since ICM's first poll of the election campaign[71]).

Peter Kellner, chairman of YouGov, has observed from his company's research that the issues on which Labour focused their campaign increased in salience during the campaign, while the ones which the Conservatives emphasised actually declined. Health, education and the economy, on which YouGov found Labour ahead on election day by, respectively, 26 points, 21 points and 33 points, each had a higher proportion of voters naming them as important in their voting decision on 5 May than they did at the start of the campaign. Meanwhile immigration, crime and tax, the Conservative issues,

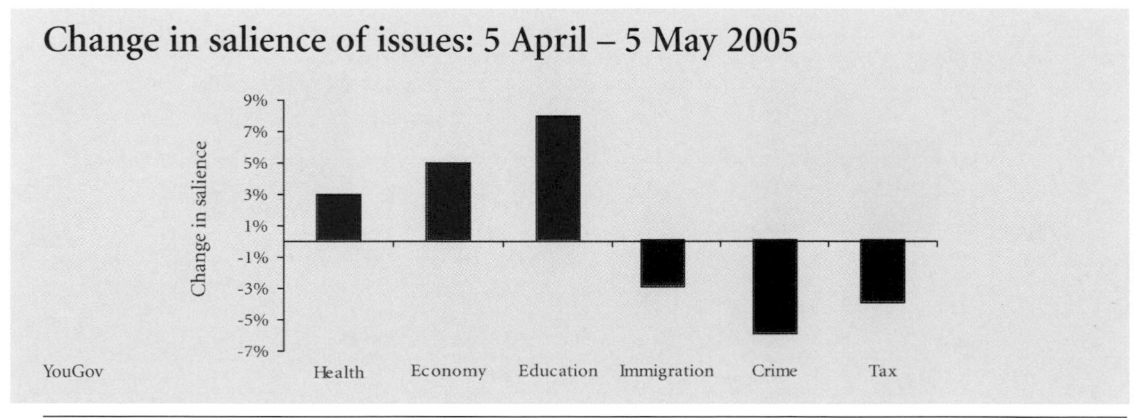

70 1-3 May 2005, sample 1,444.
71 7-8 April 2005, published in the Sunday Telegraph 9 April 2005, sample 1,012.

each declined in salience between 5 April, when the election was called, and polling day.[7] A further devastating finding that puts the Conservative lead on immigration into perspective comes from our own daily tracker. On 18-21 April, we examined the voting intentions of people who thought both that the Conservatives had the best policy on immigration and that Labour had the best policies on the economy. They intended to vote Labour by 48% to 16%.[73]

"Labour would take Britain forward, The Conservatives would take Britain back"

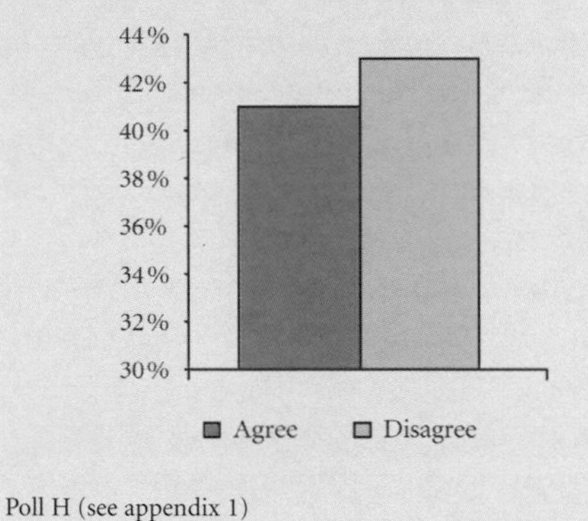

Poll H (see appendix 1)

Voters: Not Thinking What the Parties Hoped They Were Thinking

During the campaign we compared the resonance of the three main parties' election slogans in the 130 most marginal seats in which the Conservatives were in second place behind Labour[74]. Labour's rallying call, "Britain forward not back", which was also the title of the party's manifesto, was widely criticised for the

"Are you thinking what the Conservatives are thinking?"

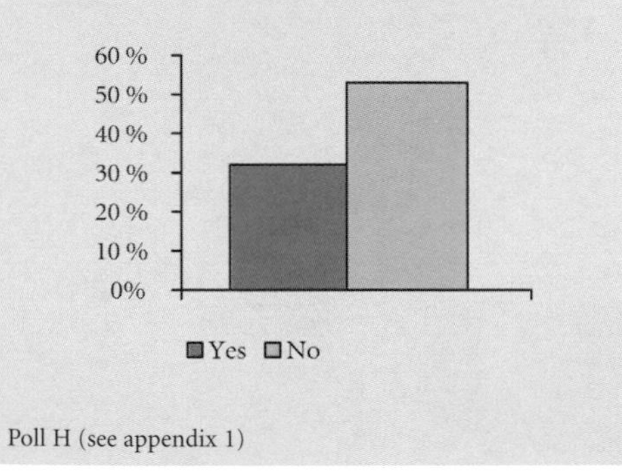

Poll H (see appendix 1)

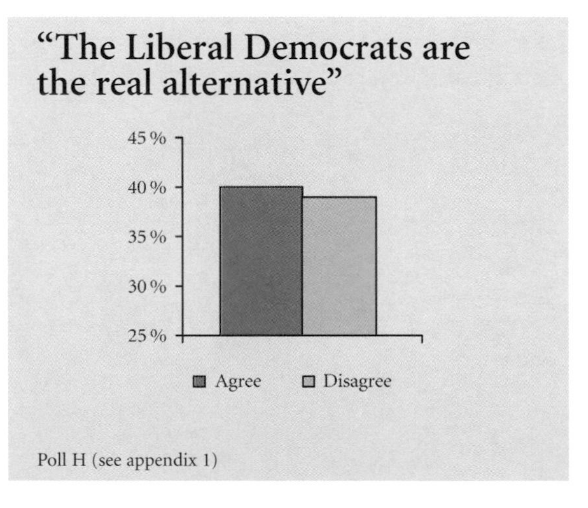

Poll H (see appendix 1)

72 YouGov polls conducted for Sky News, April 5-6, sample 1,735 and May 3-5 2005, sample 3,461.

73 Poll F: see Appendix 1.

74 Poll H: see Appendix 1.

absence of verbs. According to the poll, though, voters were fairly evenly divided as to whether it represented the reality of the choice before them. When asked if they agreed or disagreed that "under a Labour government Britain would go forwards, and that under a Conservative government it would go backwards", 41% agreed, while 43% did not.

The Conservative slogan, "are you thinking what we're thinking?", was unveiled at the end of January. It featured in a series of posters and newspaper advertisements under apparently handwritten questions or statements including "I mean, how hard is it to keep a hospital clean?" and "it's not racist to impose limits on immigration". There were reports of billboards around the country being defaced, most often with passers-by responding to the question "are you thinking what we're thinking?" with a succinctly scrawled "No".

More important, voters were not thinking what they thought the Tories were thinking. When asked "are you thinking what the Conservatives are thinking", 53% said they did not. Only 32% said they did: 3 points lower than the proportion saying they would vote Conservative in the same poll.

Extending the argument they had used throughout the parliament that they, rather than the Conservatives, were the real opposition to the Labour government, the Liberal Democrats tried to position themselves at the general election as the "real alternative". Launched in March, the slogan also served as the title of the party's manifesto. Two fifths of voters agreed that "the Liberal Democrats offer a more serious alternative than the Conservatives".

War Games

Towards the end of April Tony Blair and the government came under pressure over the war in Iraq. On 24 April the Mail on Sunday reported that the Attorney General's initial legal advice had included six caveats under which invasion might be illegal, all of which were stripped from the summary of his advice published ten days later before a crucial parliamentary debate on the war. Both the Conservatives and Liberal Democrats called for the government to publish the Attorney General's advice in full, a demand to which Downing Street acceded four days later.

Charles Kennedy suggested that the election should be regarded as a referendum on the war, the Liberal Democrats having been the only one of the three main parties to have opposed it. He also called for a full public inquiry into the conflict.

Michael Howard said on the BBC's 'Question Time' on 28 April that he would have supported the invasion even if he had known Saddam Hussein had no weapons of mass destruction, because he was "a threat to the peace of the region and a threat to the wider peace in the world" – a policy he described as "regime change plus"[75]. However, he maintained that the prime minister had misled the country

75 The Independent, 30 April 2005.

over the reasons for going to war, and used this contention as the platform for a wider attack on Mr Blair's integrity. As he put it in a speech in Hastings on 23 April, "he's only taken a stand on one thing in the last eight years - taking Britain to war. And he couldn't even tell the truth about that"[76].

In the following days the Conservatives' attacks on Mr Blair intensified, culminating on 27 April in the launch of billboard posters featuring a picture of the prime minister with the message: "If he's prepared to lie to take us to war, he's prepared to lie to win an election".

As was already clear from voters' views of the two leaders expressed in the twelve constituency polls, personal attacks on the prime minister were never likely to pay electoral dividends for the Conservatives. At the end of April ICM found for the Guardian[77] that more than half of voters (51%) did not think Mr Blair was trustworthy. Three days later they discovered for the Sunday Telegraph that two thirds of the electorate would not buy a used car from him[78].

A Populus poll for The Times conducted immediately before the poster launch[79] found that less than a quarter (24%) of voters trusted Tony Blair. The remaining three quarters were quite evenly divided between those who used to trust him but no longer did so because he had not lived up to his promises in general (26%), had lost trust because of the way he handled Iraq (22%), or had never trusted him in the first place (23%).

But at this stage in the campaign, according to the daily tracker, Labour had a 9-point lead over the Conservatives and voters preferred Mr Blair to Mr Howard as prime minister by 51% to 35%[80].

So voters had already factored their concerns about Mr Blair's honesty into their voting intention. In a nutshell, they didn't trust him but wanted him to be prime minister anyway. A campaign to persuade people that he was an habitual liar therefore seemed unlikely to win over new supporters to the Conservatives. For this Conservative approach to have had any chance of success, voters would have needed to regard Michael Howard as a decidedly more trustworthy figure than the prime minister. But the ICM poll that found 51% of voters thinking Mr Blair was not trustworthy, also recorded 42% saying the same of the opposition leader. And in a separate poll in the 130 Labour marginals,[81] 33% of voters said they trusted Mr Blair more than Mr Howard to behave in an open and honest way, with only 30% trusting Mr Howard more. When pressed, the 37% who said they trusted neither divided 56%-44% in favour of Mr Blair. Anything Mr Howard said about the prime minister's trustworthiness was always going to leave him open to charges of pots and kettles.

---

76 Conservatives.com, 23 April 2005

77 Conducted 24-26 April 2005, published in the Guardian 28 April, sample 1,547.

78 Conducted 27-29 April 2005, published in the Sunday Telegraph 1 May, sample 1,532.

79 Conducted 25-26 April 2005, published in The Times 28 April 2005, sample 714.

80 Poll F: see Appendix 1.

81 Poll G: see Appendix 1.

82 Conducted by Populus, 27-28 April 2005, published in The Times 30 April 2005, sample 130.

Immediately after the poster launch a Times poll[82] tested voters' reaction to the new Tory message. Two thirds of voters, including 69% of women, felt that if Mr Blair was a liar he was no more so than most politicians. Three quarters said the Conservatives' accusation that the prime minister was a liar would make them no less likely to vote Labour, but 44% said the tactic would make them less likely to vote Conservative. 61% agreed that "by calling Tony Blair a liar the Conservatives are just resorting to name calling and showing they have nothing positive to say to try and win people's votes". And according to the daily tracking poll, this stage in the Conservative campaign coincided with sharp dips in net agreement among voters that the party "shares my values", "has plans to deal with important problems" and "stands for action not words".

On the Doorsteps

In the 130 most marginal Labour seats in which the Conservatives claimed in October 2004 to be mounting a serious challenge, the parties' campaigns varied in their impact[83].

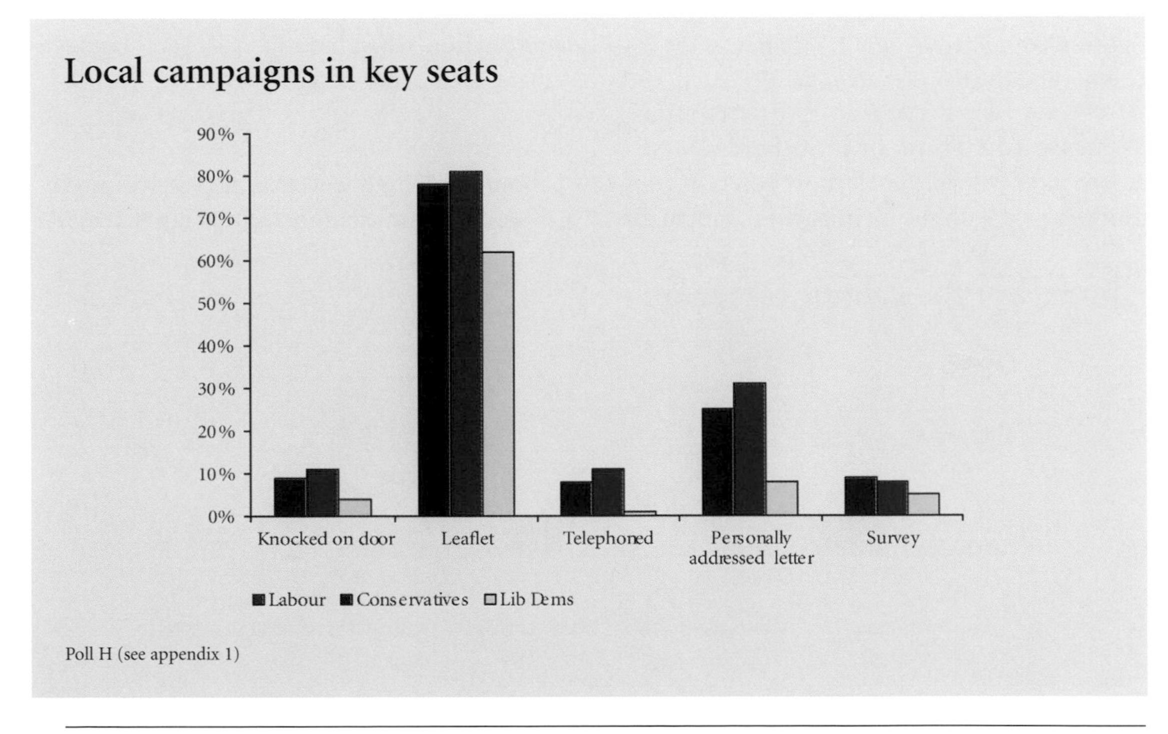

Poll H (see appendix 1)

83 Poll H: see Appendix 1.

At the end of April Labour had a slight edge over the Conservatives in most measures of local campaign activity, reaching more than four fifths (81%) of voters with leaflets and nearly a third (31%) with a personally addressed letter. Only around one voter in ten had been visited at home by each party, with similar proportions reporting having been canvassed by telephone.
In these seats Liberal Democrat voters were slightly more likely than others to have applied for a postal vote. 27% had done so, compared to 24% of Labour voters and 23% of Conservatives. The proportion of all voters who had applied for postal votes in the 40 top targets (22%) was fractionally higher than in the next tier (20%) and targets 81-130 (21%). A quarter of voters aged 55 and over intended to vote by post, compared to 20% of 18-34s and only 18% of 35-54s.

Compared with an ICM poll for the Guardian[84] conducted a few days earlier, the results suggest that proportionately more people applied for postal votes in these target seats than in the country as a whole. ICM found that 17% of voters nationally had applied for a postal vote, of whom 44% intended to vote Labour; 26% said they would support the Conservatives and 22% the Liberal Democrats. This level of postal vote applications suggested that as many as 6 million people intended to vote in this way, compared to only 1.4 million at the 2001 general election, when they divided evenly between Labour and the Conservatives at 39% each, with the Liberal Democrats securing 19%.

What do You Think of it So Far?

A few days before the election voters in the 130 Labour marginals declared themselves pretty unimpressed with the main parties' campaigns. 57% of said Labour's national campaign had made

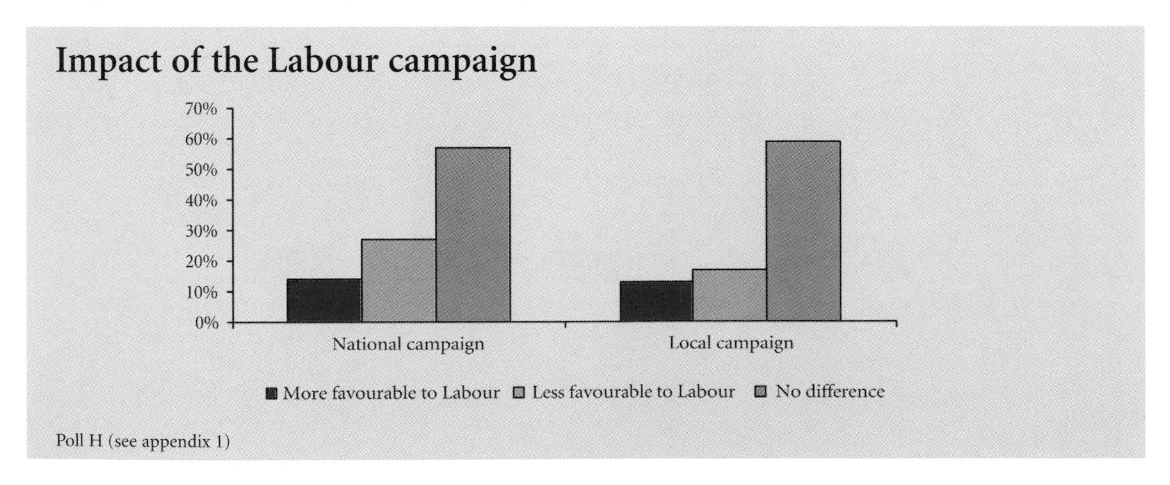

Poll H (see appendix 1)

84 Conducted 17-19 April 2005, published in the Guardian 21 April, sample 1,513.

no difference either way to their view of the party, rising to 59% for its local campaign. Only 13% and 14% respectively said the campaigns had made them more favourable to Labour, while 27% and 17% said the party's efforts had made them less favourable. More than half (51%) said Labour's campaign "offered no real vision for the future".

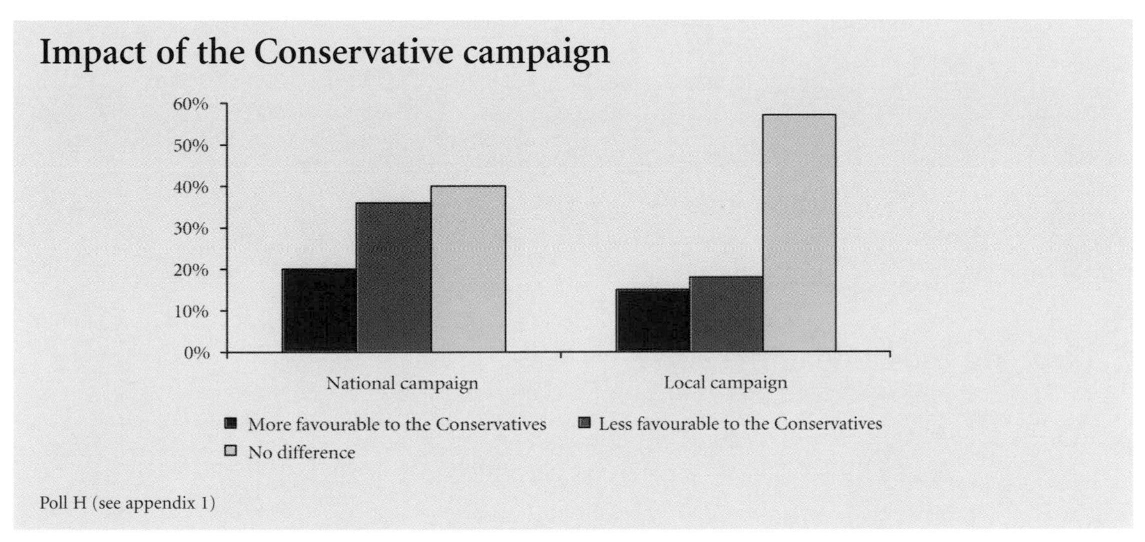

Poll H (see appendix 1)

The Conservatives' national campaign had made more of an impression on voters in these seats than Labour's. But while a fifth said it had made them more favourable to the party, more than a third (36%) said it had made them less favourable and nearly half (49%) agreed with the proposition that it was "mean, nasty and negative". Local Conservative campaigning had also made a relatively small impact, with 15% and 18% saying it had made them more and less favourable to the Tories respectively.

Although often hailed as masters of on-the-ground campaigning, the Liberal Democrats' local campaign in these seats had made even less impression than those of its rivals (though to be fair, in every constituency polled the party was in third place and was therefore deliberately deploying its resources elsewhere).

It is also notable that although relatively small, the proportions saying the local campaigns had made a positive or negative impression were by no means negligible, and could certainly be sufficient to affect the result in a close marginal seat.

The Liberal Democrats' national campaign, though, had by far the most positive impact of the three, with 30% of voters saying it had made them more favourable towards the party. It was also

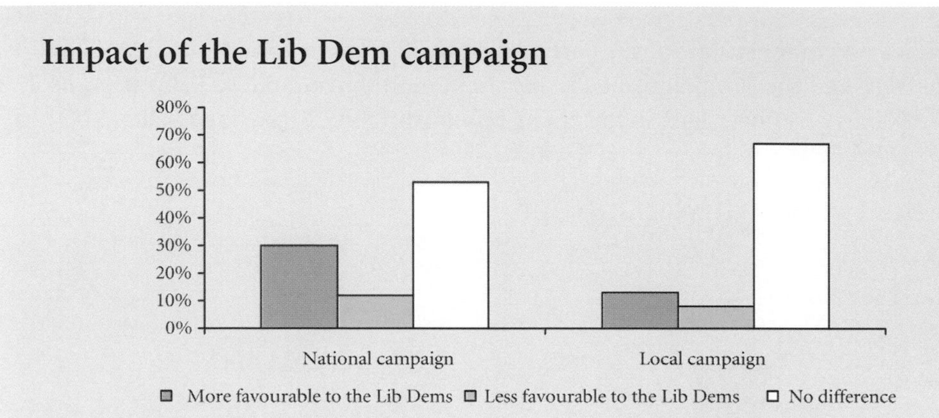

Poll H (see appendix 1)

Views on the campaign

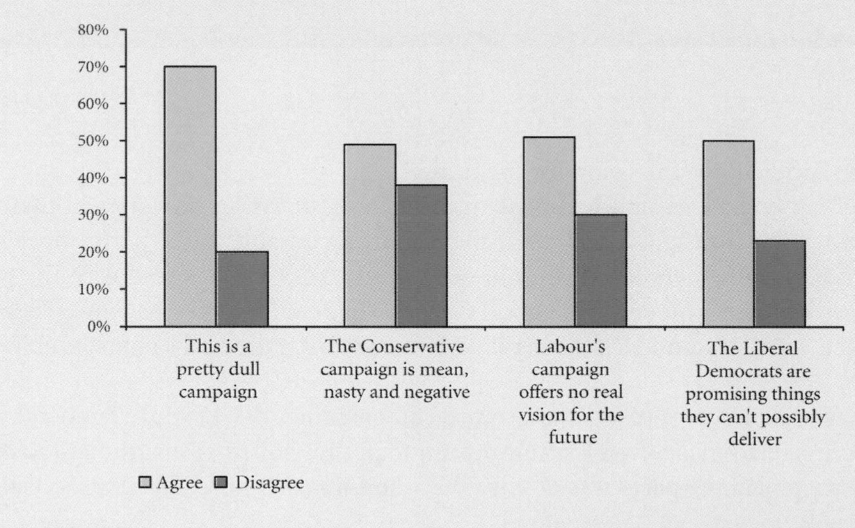

Poll H (see appendix 1)

the only campaign that made a positive impression on more people than said the opposite, even though half of voters thought the party was "promising things they can't possibly deliver".

But overall, voters felt uninspired. "This is a pretty dull campaign" was, with 70% concurring, the statement that garnered the most agreement.

Back to the Battleground: Business as Usual

With a week to go before the polling day, our research found the Conservatives trailing by an average of 5 points in the 130 constituencies that the party had defined as its battleground with Labour. Again, this was little different from the national picture – in a separate poll conducted at about the same time[85], YouGov put the Conservatives on 32%, 4 points behind.

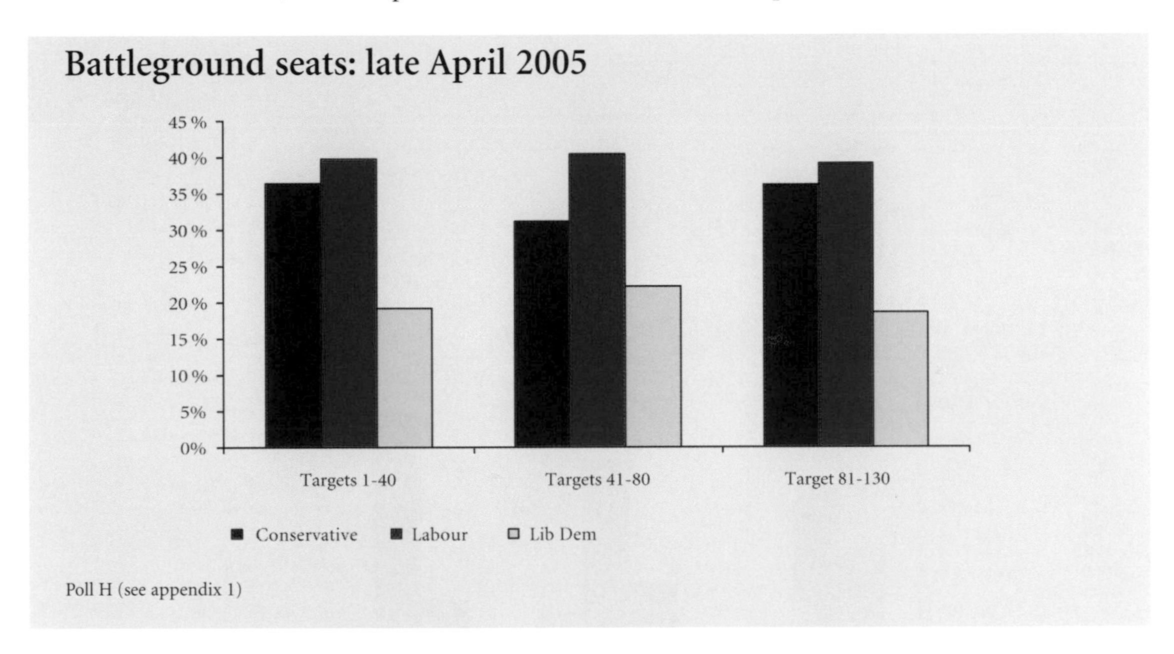

Poll H (see appendix 1)

On the battleground the Conservatives had achieved a swing of 3.5% since 2001, enough to capture just 24 seats. Even in the 40 most apparently winnable seats Labour led by 39.8%-36.4%; in targets 41-80 Labour were more than 9 points ahead, 40.4%-31.%; and Labour held a 3-point lead in the 50 most remote targets.

Between November 2004 and April 2005 the four waves of research in these 130 seats had shown little change in the parties' relative positions. Between the autumn and the spring Labour's lead across the battleground widened gradually from 3 points to 5 points.

Voters' expectations in these constituencies corresponded with their marginality. While around three quarters throughout the battleground expected a national Labour victory, only 46% in the

85 Conducted 26-28 April 2005, published in the Daily Telegraph 29 April 2005, sample 2,070.

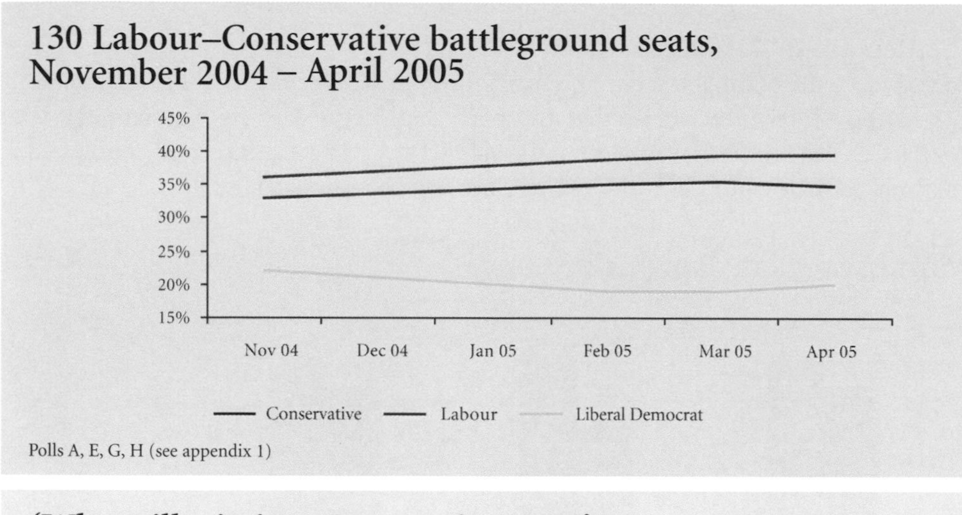

Polls A, E, G, H (see appendix 1)

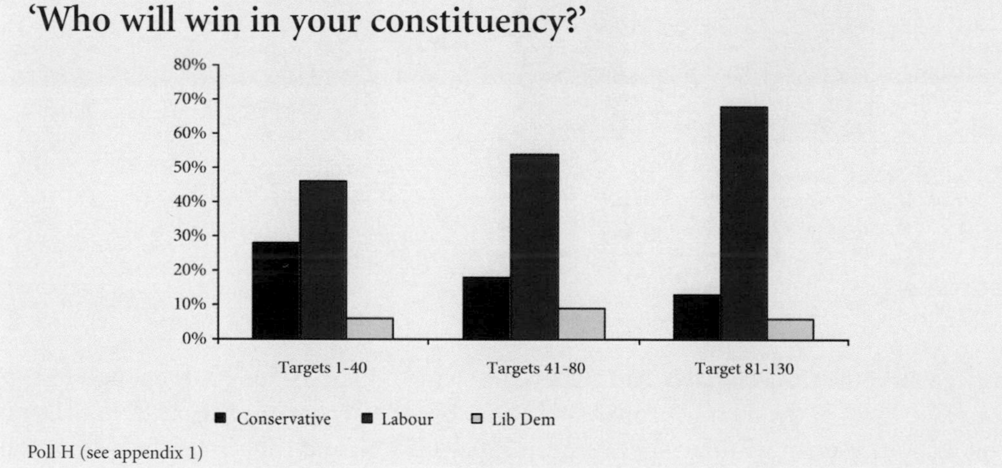

Poll H (see appendix 1)

top 40 targets expected the Labour candidate to win their seat. 54% expected a local Labour victory in the middle tier, rising to 68% in targets 81 to 130. Expectations of a Conservative victory, at only 28% even in the 40 most marginal targets, declined accordingly.

In mid-April, ICM polled a combination of 93 Labour marginals in which the Conservatives were second plus 33 Conservative-Liberal Democrat marginals held by either party[86]. In the

86 Conducted 12-14 April 2005, published in the News of the World 17 April 2005, sample 2,006.

Average of final polls

40%
35%
30%
25%
20%
15%
10%
5%
0%
Conservative
Labour
Liberal Democrats

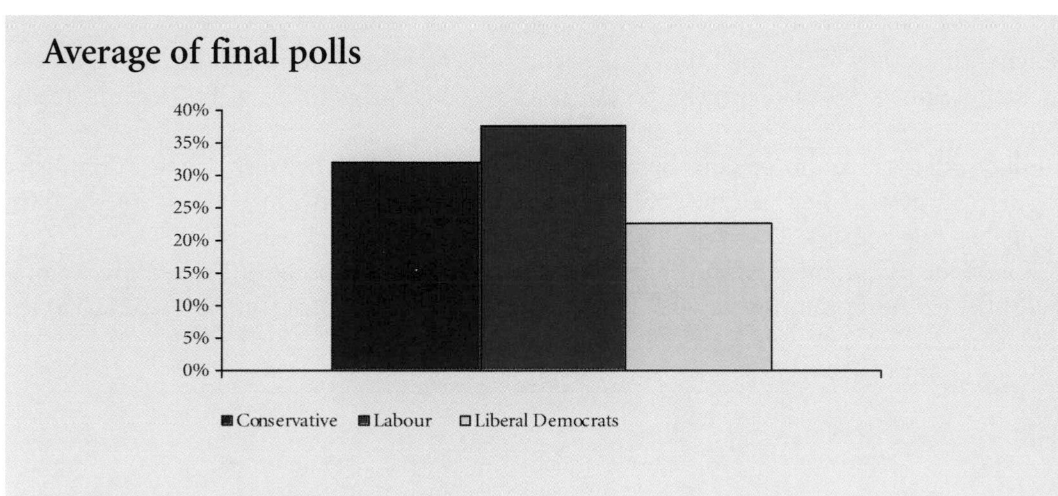

ICM, Communicate, MORI, NOP, Poulus, YouGov, May 2005

Voting intention January-May 2005

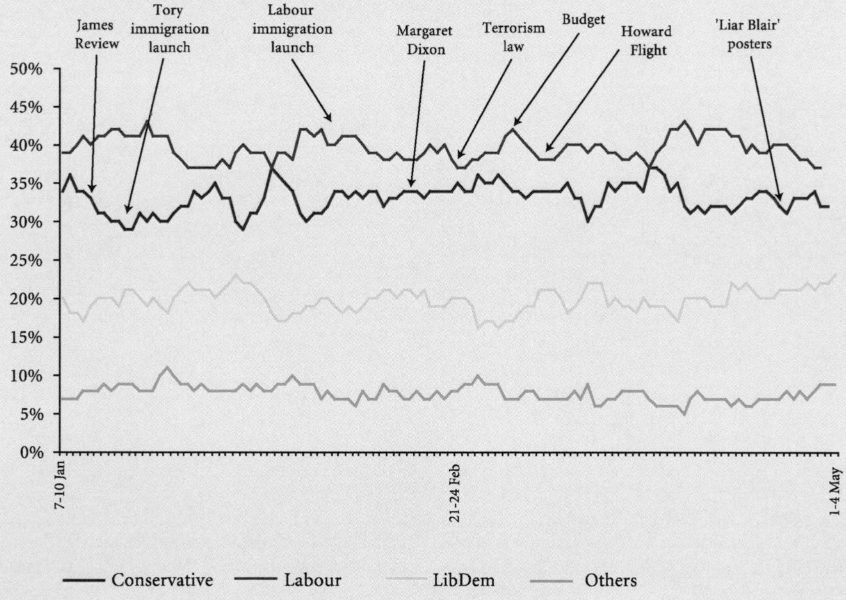

James Review
Tory immigration launch
Labour immigration launch
Margaret Dixon
Terrorism law
Budget
Howard Flight
'Liar Blair' posters
50%
45%
40%
35%
30%
25%
20%
15%
10%
5%
0%
7-10 Jan
21-24 Feb
1-4 May
Conservative
Labour
LibDem
Others

Poll F (see appendix 1)

Labour marginals they found the Conservatives on 36%, 6 points behind Labour. In the Liberal Democrat marginals, some of which the Conservatives held, the Tories were 3 points ahead, 40%-37%.

Nationally, the last round of polls before polling day, published between 1 and 5 May, gave Labour between 36% and 39% of the vote, with the Conservatives between 31% and 33% and the Liberal Democrats between 21% and 24%: a Labour lead of between 3% and 8%[87].

The final four-day segment of the daily tracker[88] was within one point of being a precise prediction of the election result. The tracker put Labour on 36%, the Conservatives on 32% and the Liberal Democrats on 23%.

In the event, the Conservatives got 33%.

---

87 ICM: L38, C32, LD22, 1-3 May, Guardian 5 May -- Communicate: L39, C31, LD 23, 23-28 April, Independent on Sunday 1 May -- MORI: L38, C33, LD23, 3-4 May, Evening Standard 5 May -- NOP: L36, C33, LD23, 1-3 May, Independent 5 May -- Populus: L38, C32, LD21, 2-3 May, Times 5 May -- YouGov: L37, C32, LD 24, 3-4 May, Daily Telegraph 5 May,

88 Poll F: see Appendix 1.

Chapter Five

What Happened, and Why

On 5 May 2005 the Labour government was returned to power with a majority of 66 seats in the House of Commons[89]. Labour won 36.2% of the vote in Great Britain, the Conservatives 33.2% and the Liberal Democrats 22.7%. Turnout was 61.3%, 2.2 points higher than in 2001.

Labour's 9.5 million votes represented the lowest share of the vote ever recorded for a winning party, and equated to only 21.6% of the electorate – another record low. The party lost 47 seats.

Tony Blair promised to respond "sensibly and wisely" to the result. "The great thing about an election," he said, "is that you get out and talk to people for week upon week and I have listened and I have learned. I think I have a very clear idea of what the British people now expect from this government for a third term."[90]

The Conservatives made a net gain of 33 seats, taking their representation in parliament to 197. Their share of the vote was 0.5% higher than in 2001. Fewer Conservative votes were cast in 2005 than in any post-war election except 2001, and the party received 800,000 fewer votes than when it was removed from government in 1997. The average Conservative share of the vote rose in seats the party won in 2001 and where they were second to the Liberal Democrats. In seats won by Labour in 2001, the Conservative share of the vote fell. The Conservatives came first in England, winning 57,000 more votes than Labour (but 93 fewer seats). However, the party's share of the vote fell in the North East, the North West, Yorkshire & Humberside the West Midlands and the East Midlands. [91]

Michael Howard said the Conservatives had taken "a significant step towards our recovery" and was proud of the Tory campaign: "We have taken a stand on the things that really do matter to the people of this country. We have sent Mr Blair a message."[92]

---

89 The final result came after the delayed election in Staffordshire South was held on 23 June as a result of the death of the Liberal Democrat candidate, Joanne Crotty. The seat was held for the Conservatives by Sir Patrick Cormack

90 BBC News Online, 6 May 2005

91 General Election 2005', Research Paper 05/33, House of Commons Library, 17 May 2005

92 BBC News Online, 6 May 2005.

MORI's aggregate examination of its general election polls[93] offered detailed analysis of how Britain had voted. While Labour and the Conservatives were tied on 34% each among men, women chose Labour by 38% to 32%. The Conservatives led among AB and C1 voters, with C2s and DEs plumping decisively for Labour. People who owned their homes outright voted Conservative by 44% to 29%, but among those with mortgages Labour won by 36% to 31%.

Aggregate analysis of general election polls

	Con	Lab	Lib Dem
All	33%	36%	23%
Gender			
Men	34%	34%	22%
Women	32%	38%	23%
Age			
18-24	28%	38%	26%
25-34	25%	38%	27%
35-44	27%	41%	23%
45-54	31%	35%	25%
55-64	39%	31%	22%
65+	41%	35%	18%
Social class			
AB	37%	28%	29%
C1	37%	32%	23%
C2	33%	40%	19%
DE	25%	48%	18%
Housing tenure			
Owned	44%	29%	20%
Mortgaged	31%	36%	25%
Social renter	16%	55%	19%
Private renter	27%	36%	28%

MORI

93 MORI Final Aggregate Analysis, sample 17,959. See mori.com

Asking for an Explanation

I commissioned two pieces of research immediately after polling day. The first was a national 'call-back' telephone survey, returning to a selection of voters who had taken part in either the comprehensive 10,000-sample poll at the beginning of the year or the daily tracker to find out why they had voted as they had, when they decided how to vote, and how they saw the parties in the aftermath of the campaign.

The second was an online survey of voters polled since November 2004 in the 130 most marginal seats in which the Conservatives had been in second place to Labour.

A sobering statistic from the national call-back poll[94] was the Conservatives' position among professionals. The proportion of people in social group ABC1 who had voted Conservative was barely 1% above the proportion saying they had voted Labour. The last time the Tories won an election they led among this section of the electorate by 32%.

Long term decline among professionals: Conservative lead among ABC1s

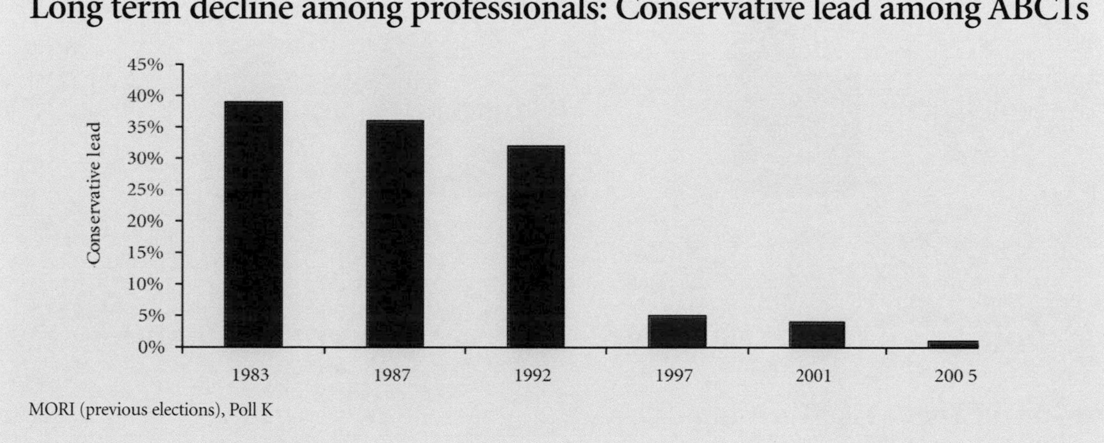

MORI (previous elections), Poll K

More than four fifths of voters (82%) said they had voted for the party they wanted to win nationally, while 18% had voted tactically. This finding was far from uniform among the parties: while 89% of those who voted Labour and 85% of those who voted Conservative had done so because they wanted the respective parties to win nationally, more than a quarter (26%) of Liberal

94 Poll K: see appendix 1

Democrat voters and 23% of floating voters had cast their ballots tactically. Nearly half of tactical voters (49%) said they were voting to stop Labour, compared to 36% who voted to block the Conservatives. Only 3% voted tactically to stop the Liberal Democrats.

Labour's national campaign was the best-received, with 28% of voters saying it made the best impression overall, 1 point ahead of the Liberal Democrats. Floating voters, although more likely to declare themselves unimpressed by any of the parties' efforts, said the Liberal Democrats' campaign had made the best impression on them. This was also true of ABs, 33% of whom agreed. The Conservative campaign received the worst reviews of the three among all groups apart from Conservative voters.

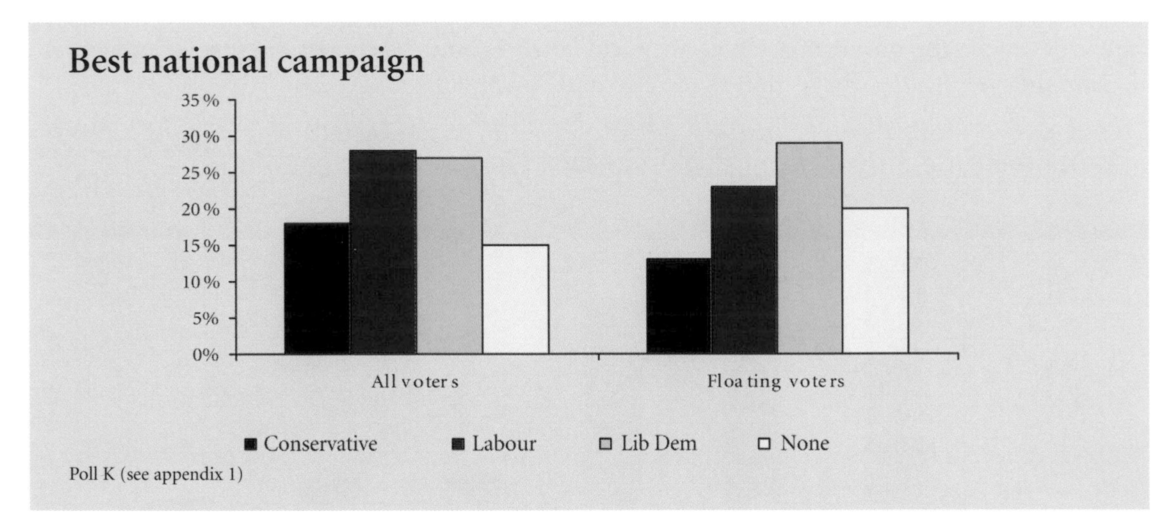

Poll K (see appendix 1)

When Did They Make Their Minds Up?

More than a third of voters (34%) had decided how they would in 2004, or even earlier than that. 15% said they had made up their minds between January and April, with a further 16% deciding in the first half of the campaign. But more than a fifth (22%) - and, perhaps by definition, half of all floating voters – remained undecided until the last couple of days before the election.

Well over half of Conservative and Labour voters had decided what to do before the election was called, with 41% and 41% respectively choosing in 2004 or earlier. Liberal Democrats made up their minds much more steadily – only 27% had decided how to vote before the beginning of the year, and nearly a quarter (23%) of those who voted Liberal Democrat decided to do so only a day or two before the election.

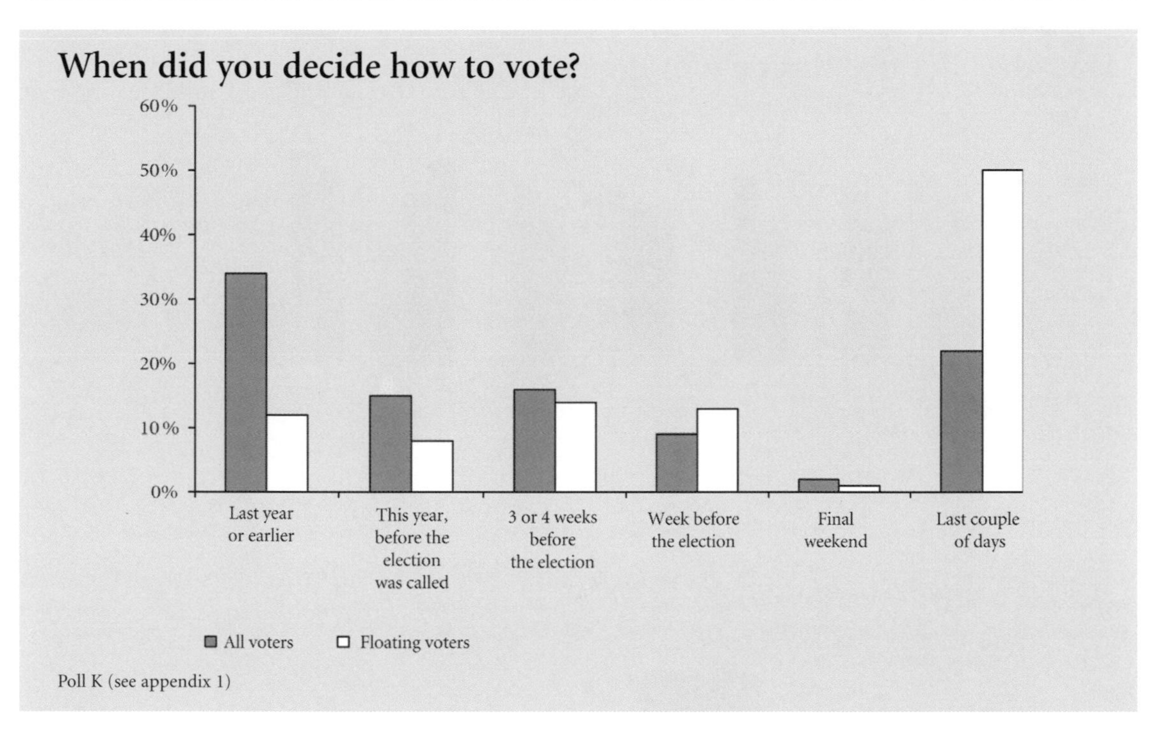

Poll K (see appendix 1)

Among people who decided how to vote in the last couple of days before the election, 33% voted Labour, 28% Liberal Democrat and 26% Conservative. Indeed, the closer to polling day people made their decisions, the less likely they were to vote Tory. While nearly 40% of voters deciding before the start of the campaign on 5 April chose the Conservatives, only 31% of those deciding in the first half of the campaign did so, falling to 27% in the week before polling day and 26% on the last weekend and thereafter. Labour and the Liberal Democrats managed to convert people at a fairly steady rate throughout the year, though only 15% of those who had made up their minds before January had decided on Charles Kennedy's party.

Those who decided not to vote would, had they actually voted, have chosen Labour over the Conservatives by 48% to 21%, while 23% would have voted Liberal Democrat. This suggests that the Conservatives turned out a higher proportion of their supporters than did the other parties. It may also be the case that had they anticipated a close result (rather than the Labour victory that was widely expected even in marginal seats, according to our polls), many of this 41% would have turned out for Labour after all. The higher the turnout, the worse the result would have been for the Conservatives.

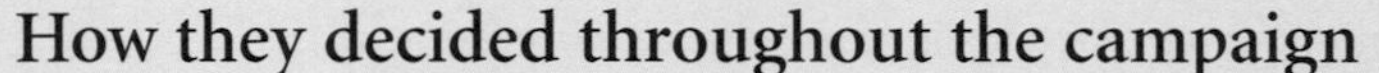

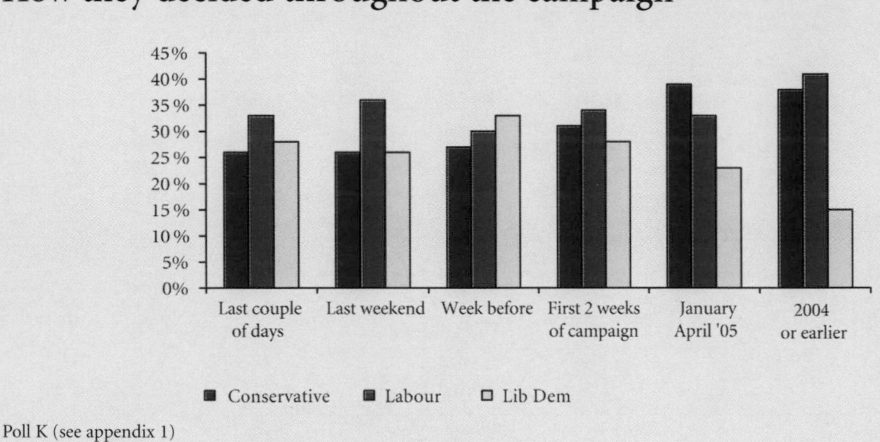

Poll K (see appendix 1)

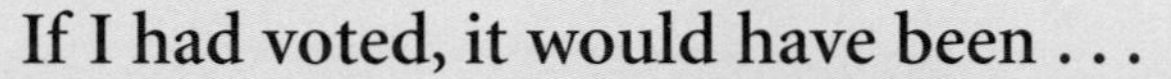

Poll K (see appendix 1)

Voting Conservative: Unthinkable?

Voters who had not voted Conservative were very evenly divided as to whether they could ever see themselves doing so: 49% said they could, 48% that they could not. This represents a fractional

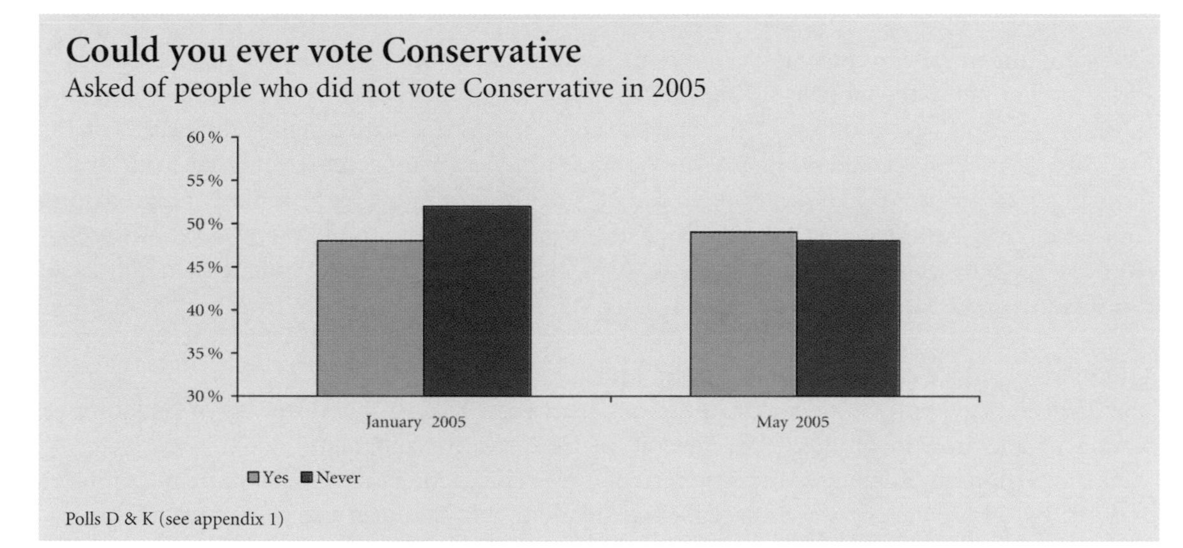

Polls D & K (see appendix 1)

"Could you see yourself voting Conservative in the future?"

Asked of non-Conservative voters

	Yes	No
All	49%	48%
Gender		
Men	51%	46%
Women	47%	50%
Age		
18-24	53%	44%
25-34	52%	46%
35-44	48%	50%
45-54	49%	49%
55-64	49%	47%
65+	44%	51%
Social class		
AB	53%	44%
C1	49%	48%
C2	50%	47%
DE	43%	53%

Polls K (see appendix 1)

increase in the number of potential Conservative voters since our 10,000-sample poll in January[95], and a 4-point fall in the number saying they could never see themselves voting for the party.

Younger people were relatively open to the idea of voting Conservative in the future (53% of 18-24s and 52% of 25-34s could see themselves doing so), as were people in the South East (55%) and those in social group AB (53% - although the 44% of this group unable to see themselves voting Tory in the future present a serious challenge in the party's task of rebuilding the level of support required to win general elections). Only 47% of women said they might one day vote Conservative, compared to 51% of men.

The Conservative campaign: facing the facts

The daily tracking poll,[96] conducted continuously between 7 January and the eve of poll, offered an inescapable measure of the effectiveness of the Conservative campaign.

At the beginning of January voters preferred Tony Blair to Michael Howard as prime minister by 13%; by 4 May the gap was 14%. Labour extended their lead over the Conservatives on tax, managing the economy, spending taxpayers' money well and improving public services. The Conservatives turned a 2% deficit on crime into a 5% lead, and were ahead on immigration by 17% in January and 16% in May. At the beginning of January 34% intended to vote Conservative; on 5 May 33% did so.

The national follow-up poll found that 44% of all those who did not vote Conservative – including identical proportions of men, women and ABs, and within one point of the levels in other social groups – agreed that they were "seriously considering doing so but were put off by how the Conservatives came across during the campaign". Just over half (52%) disagreed.

What Put Them Off?

As in the January poll, our national follow-up survey asked people who did not vote Conservative but could see themselves doing so some time in the future about their reasons for not voting Conservative.

The most widespread criticism remained that the Conservatives "don't have any strong leaders", a statement with which 68% agreed – the same proportion as at the beginning of the year. There was some variation in view between age groups, with only 59% of 18-24s inclined to agree compared to 74% of those aged 55-64.

Close behind was the proposition that "they come across as opportunist – just opposing whatever Labour does and saying whatever they think might be popular". Nearly two-thirds (64%) agreed with this, down 1 point since January.

95 Poll D: see Appendix 1.

96 Poll F: see Appendix 1.

Changes in daily tracker poll findings: January-May 2005

	7-10 Jan	1-4 May
Conservative voting intention	34%	32%
Preference of prime minister Tony Blair	48%	50%
Michael Howard	35%	36%
Conservative lead on:		
The amount of tax ordinary people pay	-2%	-7%
Managing the economy in good times and bad	-17%	-23%
Spending taxpayers' money well	-3%	-15%
Improving public services	-18%	-20%
Dealing properly with crime	-2%	5%
Getting a grip on immigration & asylum	17%	16%
Britain's approach to the EU	-7%	-9%
The Conservatives party:		
Shares my values	-16%	-15%
Would do a good job in government	-5%	-9%
Has plans to deal with the most important issues	-12%	-6%
Stands for action not words	-9%	-13%

Polls F (see appendix 1)

The criticism that the party was "too dominated by men" remained prominent, although the proportion agreeing had fallen from 60% to 49% since January. Well over half of women (56%) agreed with the proposition, compared to 42% of men.

Although 46% of non-Conservative voters who could see themselves voting Conservative in the future said the party was not "promising bold enough cuts in tax and the size of government", down 1 point since January, 45% disagreed with the proposition. While women and voters aged 18-44 agreed with the statement by margins of between 4 and 8 points, men and people aged 45 and over rejected it. Voters in social groups ABC1 also disagreed (ABs by 52%-40%), as did floating voters (46%-43%).

The proportions saying the Conservatives "don't seem to stand for anything any more" and "just don't seem to have anything relevant to say about the problems facing the country today" had both fallen to 40% (from 47% and 49% respectively). Both propositions were rejected by decisive margins particularly among the youngest voters, with 69% of 18-24s disagreeing with each.

What is wrong with the Tories

Asked of people who did not vote Conservative in 2005 but could see themselves doing so in the future

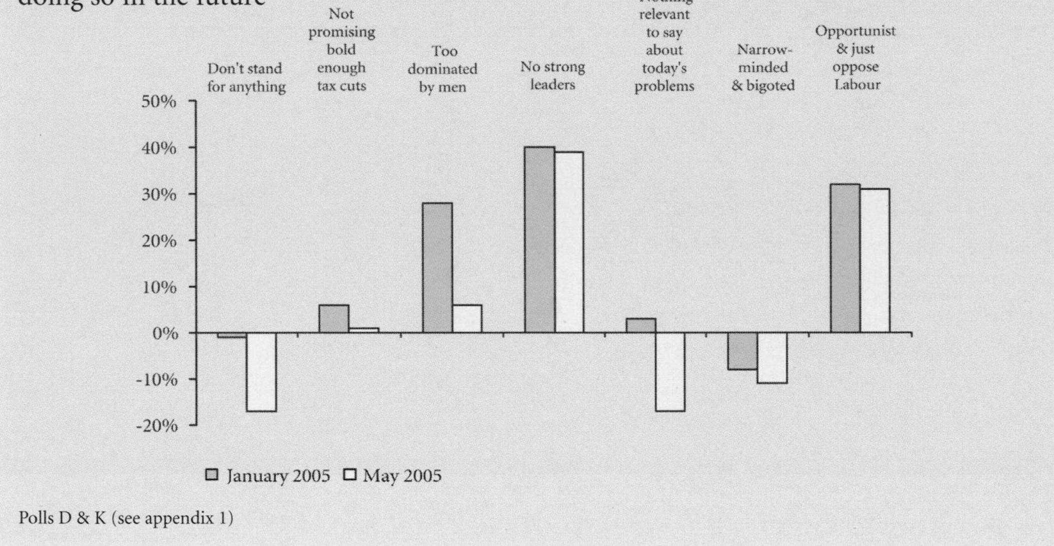

Polls D & K (see appendix 1)

Just under two fifths (29%) considered the party "narrow minded and bigoted about issues like gay rights and racial equality" – 1 point down on January – but again the proposition was rejected by all groups, including the 18-24s (51%-39%) and ABs (50%-42%) who had tended to express in the January poll the most socially liberal views on issues such as racial and religious diversity and gay rights.

What Have They Got That We Haven't

Between January and May 2005 the proportion of voters saying the Liberal Democrats shared their values rose from 41% to 52%, overtaking Labour, for whom the proportion increased from 43% to 49%. The Conservatives registered the smallest increase over the period, from 34% to 36%. Uniquely, more people disagreed than agreed that the Conservatives shared their values, with 60% saying the party did not. The margin of disagreement was particularly wide among floating voters, who disagreed by 62%-35%, and younger voters: 25-34 year-olds disagreed by 65%-31%.

Voters as a whole agreed that Labour shared their values, with the exception of those aged 55 and over, ABs, and people in the South East and the Midlands. All groups accepted the proposi-

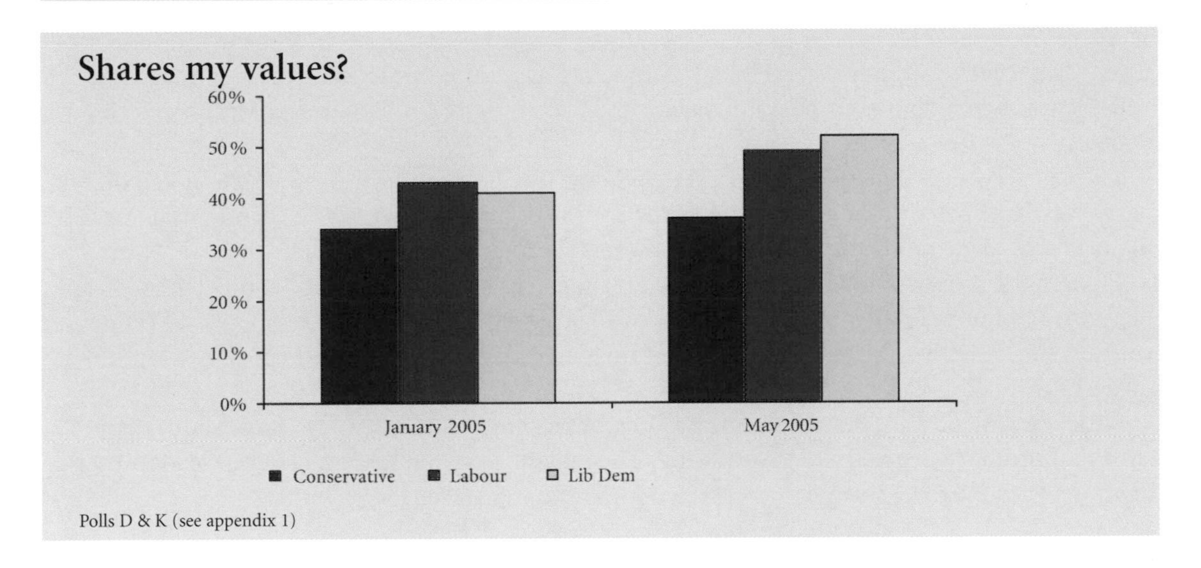

Polls D & K (see appendix 1)

tion in the case of the Liberal Democrats, with voters overall agreeing by 52%-41%. Agreement was particularly marked among floating voters (56%-38%) ABs (56%-40%).

There was a marked increase in the proportion of voters regarding the Labour Party as "competent and capable" between January and the election. A clear majority of all groups agreed (apart

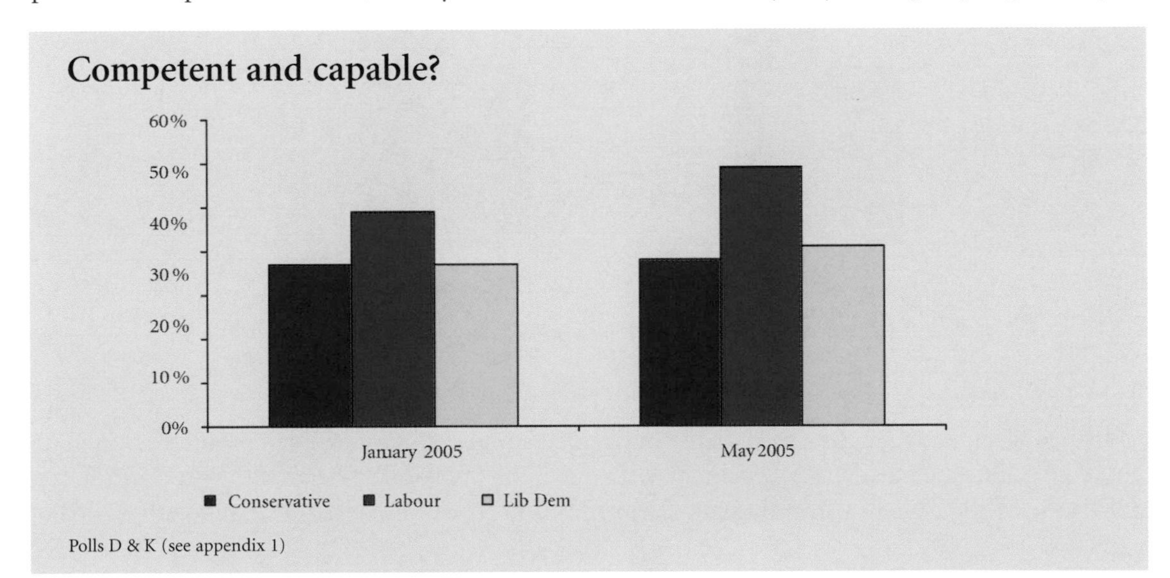

Polls D & K (see appendix 1)

from Conservative supporters – Liberal Democrats agreed by more than the national average), with 59% supporting the proposition overall and 38% rejecting it. Floating voters agreed by 60% to 36%.

The Conservatives' figures were almost exactly the reverse of Labour's: only 38% agreed that the party was "competent and capable" (1 point up since January), with 57% demurring. Decisive majorities in all groups except Conservative voters disagreed with the proposition.

Though the proportion of Liberal Democrat voters regarding the party as "competent and capable" rose 4 points over the period, a majority of all groups disagreed (apart from Liberal Democrat voters – but only two thirds of them agreed the party was competent and capable. More than a quarter 26% said it was not).

Little movement was recorded in the proportions saying that each party "cares about the problems that ordinary people have to deal with". The Liberal Democrats were the clear leaders on this measure, with overall agreement at 62%, a 30-point margin over the dissenters.

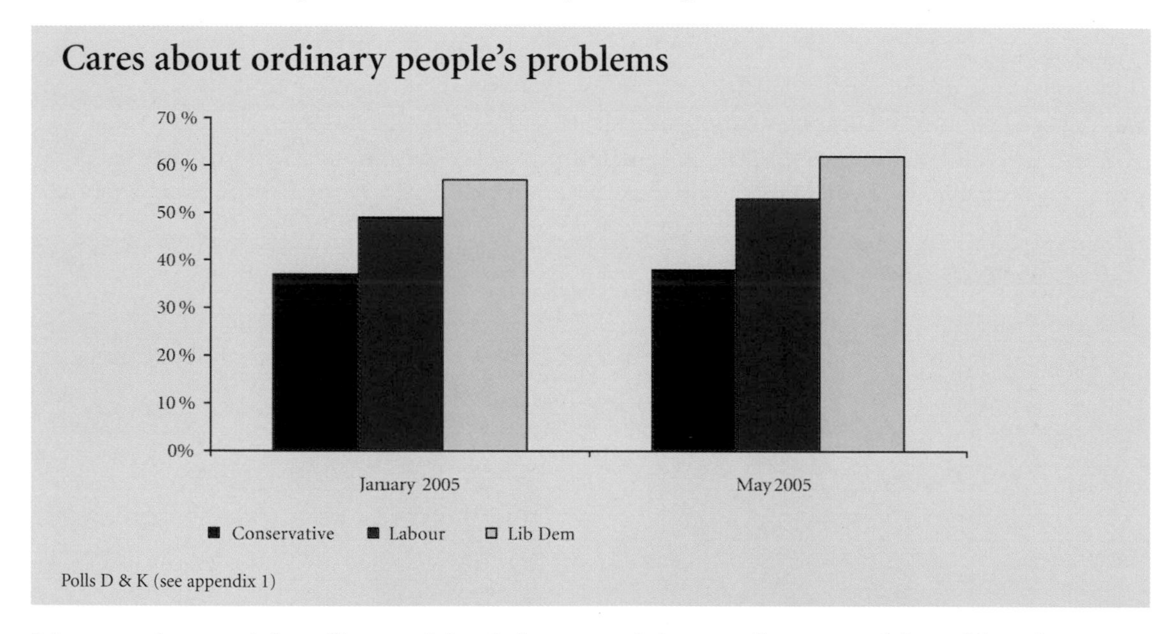

Polls D & K (see appendix 1)

More people agreed than disagreed that Labour cared about ordinary people's problems by a margin of 10 points higher than disagreement, with only 55-64 year-olds rejecting the proposition (by 52%-45%). Only 38% of voters thought the proposition true of the Conservatives, with 57% disagreeing.

Agreement that the parties "will deliver what they promise if elected" rose slightly in each case between January and the election. However, it was notable that in no case did more than half of voters expect a party to keep its word, and floating voters had less confidence in each party's promises than voters as a whole. For Labour and the Conservatives, the only groups among whom more people expected promises to be kept than broken were their own supporters.

The Liberal Democrats were closer to being trusted on this score. Overall their expectation gap was only 2 points (compared to 14 points for Labour and 24 points for the Conservatives, whom voters expected to break their promises by 58% to 34%) and some groups, on balance, expected Charles Kennedy's party to deliver: women (by 44%-42%), 18-24s (by 46%-44%), ABs (by 46%-42%) and C1s (by 46%-43%), and people in Wales and the South West (45%-44%) and Scotland (47%-44%).

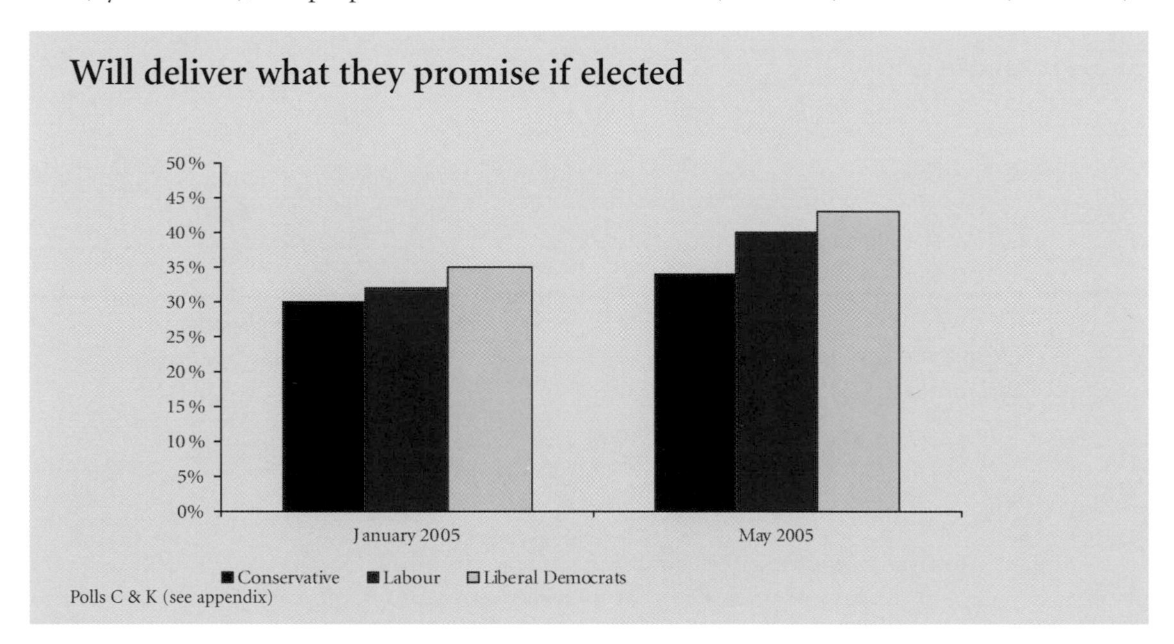

Polls C & K (see appendix)

What Conservative Voters Made of it All

Our follow-up survey asked people who had voted Conservative whether or not they agreed with a selection of statements, and compared their answers with those of Conservative supporters in Tory-Liberal Democrat marginals recorded in December 2004.[97]

97 Polls C & K: see Appendix 1.

Although not based on a direct comparison (the follow-up poll having used a national sample), Conservative voters appear to have considered the election result a cause for optimism. Fewer than one in ten Conservatives now thought the party was "on its last legs" (down from 12% to 8%), and the proportion thinking the state of the party had got worse since Michael Howard became leader had halved, to 11%. Nearly a third (30%) still felt that "the Conservative Party has not really changed at all since it lost power in 1997", down from 38%, and 72% now said they could sum up clearly to a friend what the Conservative Party stood for, up 10 points since December.

In addition, the May follow-up poll asked whether Conservatives were "worried that the Liberal Democrats may now come to be seen as the main opposition to Labour". Less than a quarter (24%) harboured such a fear; 74% said they did not.

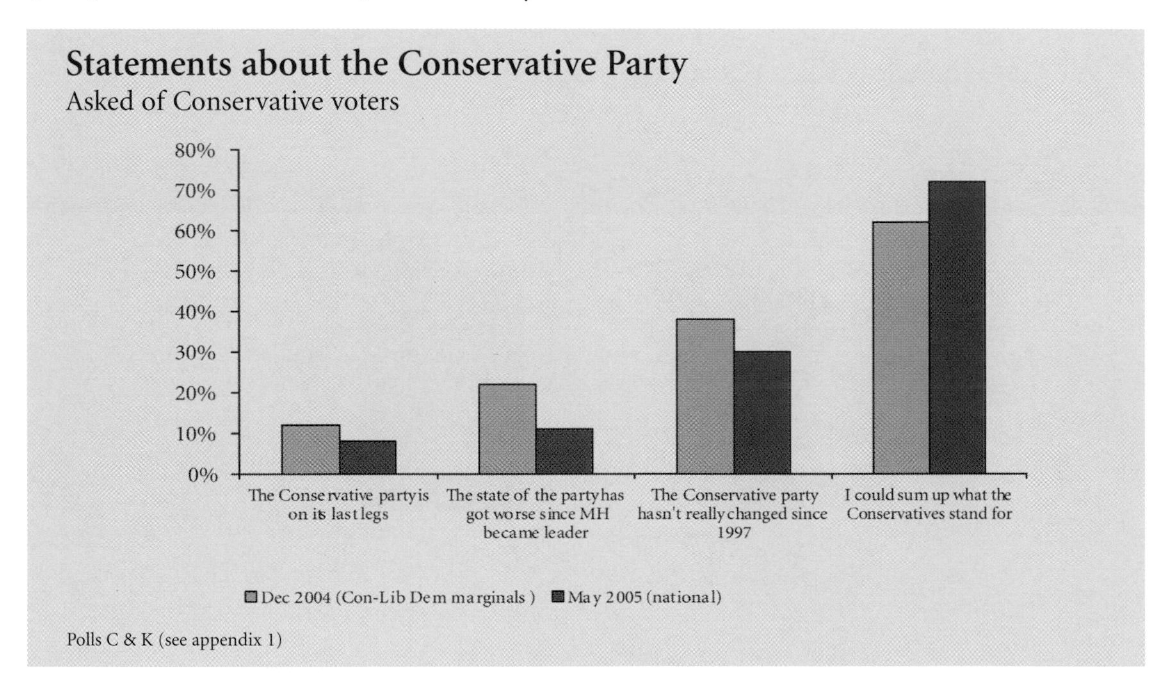

Polls C & K (see appendix 1)

Back to the Battleground: Counting the Casualties

The Conservatives won 30 of the 130 seats the party had defined as its battleground with Labour in England and Wales: 26 of their top 40 Labour targets; 3 of the next 40, and only 1 of the most ambitious 50. The national swing from Labour to the Conservatives was 3.15%. This should have been enough to topple the 22 seats where Labour had a majority of 6.3% or less. However, the

Conservatives won only 17 of these seats, and would not have done so in 7 had it not been for Labour voters switching to the Liberal Democrats (or in the case of Hornchurch, the BNP and others, or in Northampton South, a range of smaller parties) whose vote increased by more than the resulting Conservative majority. In one, Shipley, the Conservative share of the vote was lower than in 2001.

Of the 13 Conservative gains where Labour's majority had been greater than 6.3%, only two – Peterborough and Putney – were a result of a direct Labour-Conservative swing. In the remaining 11, the increase in the Liberal Democrat vote was greater than the resulting Conservative majority. The Liberal Democrat vote increased by more than the Conservative vote in 15 of the top 22 and 22 of the top 30 Labour targets following the national pattern in which the Conservative vote fell overall in seats Labour were defended, while the Lib Dem share rose by more than 5%, with the consequence that the Lib Dems overtook the Conservatives in 80 of seats and are now second to Labour in only 80 fewer seats than the Conservatives.

In their 130 target Labour seats the Conservatives achieved an average swing of 3.55% from Labour - almost precisely that measured in our final pre-election battleground poll.

In the top 40 targets the swing was 3.59%, and in the next tranche, numbers 41-80, it was 3.17% - hardly distinguishable from the national average of 3.15%.

The swing in targets 81-130 was marginally better at 3.83%, but given the Labour majorities this far down the list the difference is neither here nor there. If the Conservatives had decided against targeting the 50 most ambitious seats on their list, but had achieved a 2-point improvement in the average swing on the remainder of the list, they would have won nearly twice as many Labour seats as they did. (It is true that one of the most ambitious target seats, Enfield Southgate, did fall to the Conservatives. It would not have done so, though, had a sizeable proportion of Labour voters not switched to the Liberal Democrats. And taking nothing away from the Conservative candidate

Labour-Conservative swings required and achieved

	Required	Achieved
National		3.15%
Top 130 most marginal Labour seats		3.55%
Of which		
1-40 (most marginal)		3.59%
41-80		3.17%
81-130		3.83%

David Burrowes, who fought a first-rate campaign, his achievement in dislodging the education minister Stephen Twigg was all the more remarkable for being so unexpected).

The Conservative performance in the battleground seats can only have been disappointing for the party, particularly when compared with the co-chairman's October 2004 report that the Conservatives were then in the lead in no fewer than 103 of these seats. The most likely explanation for this discrepancy, supported by published evidence and our own research, is that the Tories were never in the winning position their leadership thought, and that by designating such a large number of targets the party adopted a disastrous strategy.

The party used scarce resources campaigning heavily in constituencies that it had no realistic prospect of winning; therefore it failed to win not only those constituencies, but others higher up the list where it might have had a real chance of victory.

For example, the Conservatives won two seats in Yorkshire out of a total of 16 targets. Had they not directed money and people to Leeds North East and Wakefield, where Labour were defending majorities of 17% and more, they would surely have had a better chance of capturing Elmet, Calder Valley and Selby (which they lost by 467 votes, having needed a swing of less than 2.2%).

Of the 34 seats in their chosen battleground with the Liberal Democrats, the Conservatives won only five. While the party never put a figure on the number of Liberal Democrat seats it was poised to reclaim, the fact that so many constituencies were targeted, some with large majorities, may again account for the fact that more plausible targets (including 5 that required a swing of 1% or less) were not captured.

Of the three targets in Hampshire, the Conservatives came within 125 votes of gaining Romsey and 568 votes of gaining Eastleigh. Had the party deployed to these seats the people and resources it used in Winchester, which required a swing of more than 8% (and the Liberal Democrats held with a majority of 7,467), one or both of them might have fallen. In the event, it lost all three.

Far from being a plucky and heroic but ultimately unsuccessful attempt to confound expectations, the Conservatives' targeting strategy was a disaster waiting to happen. The purpose of selecting targets is to maximise the number of seats gained with the level of resources available. The Tories' scattergun approach produced precisely the opposite result.

The Campaign in Retrospect

Among the first people to offer a critique of the Conservative campaign was the party co-chairman, Lord Saatchi. The weekend after election he wrote: "the mere promise of efficiency is not enough to persuade people that you would be an efficient government. Mere anger at the problems of the world we live in is not enough to convince the voters that the Conservative Party is fit to solve them". Though the party made clear what it did not like about modern Britain, "we did not raise the horizons of the British people and tell them with sufficient optimism, excitement and passion what 'should be'. This

Target seats: Labour and Lib Dem with 2001 majorites

1	South Dorset	0.3
2	Braintree	0.7
3	Monmouth	0.9
4	Lancaster & Wyre	0.9
5	Kettering	1.2
6	Northampton South	1.7
7	Welwyn Hatfield	2.8
8	Shipley	3.1
9	Clwyd West	3.2
10	Bexleyheath & Crayford	3.6
11	North East Milton Keynes	3.9
12	Hornchurch	4.2
13	Selby	4.3
14	Hammersmith & Fulham	4.5
15	South Thanet	4.5
16	Forest of Dean	4.6
17	Wellingborough	4.6
18	Ilford North	5.3
19	Rugby & Kenilworth	5.3
20	Gillingham	5.4
21	Harwich	5.4
22	Enfield North	6
23	Calder Valley	6.5
24	Redditch	6.7
25	Peterborough	7.2
26	Shrewsbury & Atcham	7.2
27	Dartford	7.4
28	Scarborough & Whitby	7.5
29	Hove	7.6
30	Preseli Pembrokeshire	8
31	Gloucester	8
32	Putney	8.1
33	Hemel Hempstead	8.2
34	South Ribble	8.2
35	Finchley & Golder's Green	8.5
36	Wolverhampton South West	8.5
37	The Wrekin	8.6
38	Croydon Central	8.7
39	Elmet	9.1
40	Wimbledon	9.1
41	Stroud	9.1
42	Keighley	9.2
43	Sittingbourne & Sheppey	9.3
44	High Peak	9.3
45	Stourbridge	9.5
46	Brigg & Goole	9.6
47	Falmouth & Camborne	9.7
48	Medway	9.8
49	Colne Valley	9.9
50	Wirral West	10
51	St Albans	10.2
52	Vale of Glamorgan	10.4
53	Burton	10.4
54	Hastings & Rye	10.5
55	Pendle	10.8
56	Bradford West	10.9
57	Chatham & Aylesford	10.9
58	Warwick & Leamington	11.1
59	Gravesham	11.1
60	Great Yarmouth	11.3
61	Wansdyke	11.3
62	Stafford	11.3
63	Tamworth	11.4
64	Dover	11.6
65	Rossendale & Darwen	11.9
66	Watford	12
67	Broxtowe	12
68	Corby	12.1
69	Morecambe & Lunesdale	12.2
70	Carmarthen West & South Pembrokeshire	12.3
71	Leeds North West	12.3
72	Birmingham Edgbaston	12.4
73	Pudsey	12.5
74	Brighton Kemptown	12.6
75	Wirral South	12.7
76	Gedling	12.8
77	Reading East	12.8
78	Norwich North	12.9
79	Harlow	13
80	Worcester	13
81	Batley & Spen	13.1
82	Harrow West	13.2
83	Enfield Southgate	13.2
84	Cleethorpes	13.2
85	Bolton West	13.4
86	Blackpool North & Fleetwood	13.4
87	Staffordshire Moorlands	13.7
88	Battersea	13.7
89	Portsmouth North	13.9
90	Cardiff North	14.3
91	Erewash	14.3
92	Copeland	14.3
93	Loughborough	14.4
94	Bury North	14.6
95	South Derbyshire	15.1
96	Bedford	15.2
97	Halifax	15.2
98	City of Chester	15.4
99	Milton Keynes South West	15.4
100	Derby North	15.8
101	Amber Valley	16.2
102	Warrington South	16.3
103	Carlisle	16.3
104	South Swindon	16.9
105	Crawley	17.1
106	Nuneaton	17.4
107	Chorley	17.6
108	Dudley North	17.6
109	Vale of Clwyd	17.8
110	Leeds North East	17.8
111	Conwy	18.1
112	North West Leicestershire	18.1
113	Waveney	18.1
114	Hendon	18.2
115	Halesowen & Rowley Regis	18.7
116	Dudley South	18.8
117	Basildon	18.9
118	Northampton North	19
119	North Swindon	19.1
120	Plymouth Sutton	19.2
121	Wakefield	19.3
122	Tynemouth	19.8
123	Gower	19.8
124	Birmingham Hall Green	20.1
125	Stevenage	20.2
126	Dewsbury	20.3
127	Sherwood	20.4
128	Stockton South	20.6
129	Coventry South	20.6
130	Norwich South	20.7

Held by Labour
Gained by Conservatives
Gained by Lib Dems

1	Cheadle	0.08
2	Weston-Super-Mare	0.72
3	Norfolk North	0.86
4	Dorset Mid & Poole North	0.88
5	Guildford	1.12
6	Somerton & Frome	1.27
7	Brecon & Radnorshire	2
8	Devon West & Torridge	2.14
9	Hereford	2.17
10	Ludlow	3.78
11	Newbury	4.75
12	Romsey	4.89
13	Teignbridge	5.08
14	Devon North	6.06
15	Eastleigh	6.43
16	Southport	7.31
17	Yeovil	8.16
18	Richmond Park	10.1
19	Cornwall South East	10.39
20	Sutton & Cheam	10.84
21	Carshalton & Wallington	11.2
22	Cheltenham	12.56
23	Colchester	12.7
24	Torbay	14.1
25	Twickenham	15.33
26	Portsmouth South	15.54
27	Truro & St Austell	16.04
28	Winchester	16.29
29	Northavon	17.71
30	Oxford West & Abingdon	17.81
31	Cornwall North	18.21
32	St Ives	20.41
33	Harrogate & Knaresborough	20.97
34	Bath	21.37

Held by Lib Dems
Gained by Conservatives

was a tragedy of failed communication and false perception because no Tory politician cares more about 'what should be' than Michael Howard". He declared that "a clear sense of purpose, a certain idealism, a marching tune people can respond to, is, as it once was for Disraeli, Churchill and Thatcher, the essential precondition for success – the only way to make this the next Conservative century".[98]

Our final round of research[99], conducted after the election in the 130 Labour battleground seats, provided some interesting perspectives on these observations.

Voters in these seats regarded the Conservative campaign as "negative" rather than "positive" by 41% to 15%, and nearly four times as many voters saw it as "aggressive" (38%) as considered it "moderate" (10%). Voters aged 18-34 and those in social groups ABC1 were more likely than voters as a whole to have thought the Conservative campaign negative and aggressive, and only 38% of Conservative voters believed the party's campaign had been positive. More than twice as many voters regarded it as "confused" (30%) as thought it had been "clear" (13%), and while less than a fifth described it as "sloppy", only 13% considered it "professional". While more than a quarter found the Tory campaign "depressing", only one voter in 25 found it "uplifting".

Characteristics of the campaigns

	Con	Lab	Lib Dem
Positive	15%	24%	36%
Negative	41%	24%	8%
Aggressive	38%	20%	4%
Moderate	10%	20%	32%
Clear	13%	16%	21%
Confused	30%	29%	23%
Professional	13%	20%	17%
Sloppy	19%	19%	12%
Uplifting	4%	4%	10%
Depressing	27%	25%	10%

Poll L (see appendix 1)

98 Sunday Telegraph, 8 May 2005.
99 Conducted by YouGov 10-14 May 2005, sample 4,592.

The most widely chosen phrase to describe how the Conservatives had come across during the campaign was "old fashioned". More than six times as many people selected this description (43%) as chose "modern" (7%). Only 14% had seen the party as "trustworthy", compared to more than a quarter (26%) who thought it had come across as "dishonest". Nearly a fifth of voters (18%) thought the Conservatives seemed "normal", but more than one in ten (11%) regarded them as "weird". Only half as many voters thought the party appeared "concerned about people like me" (17%) as thought it was "not concerned about people like me", and while a fifth believed the Conservatives were "in it for what they believe is best for the country", more than a third (36%) thought they were "in it only for themselves".

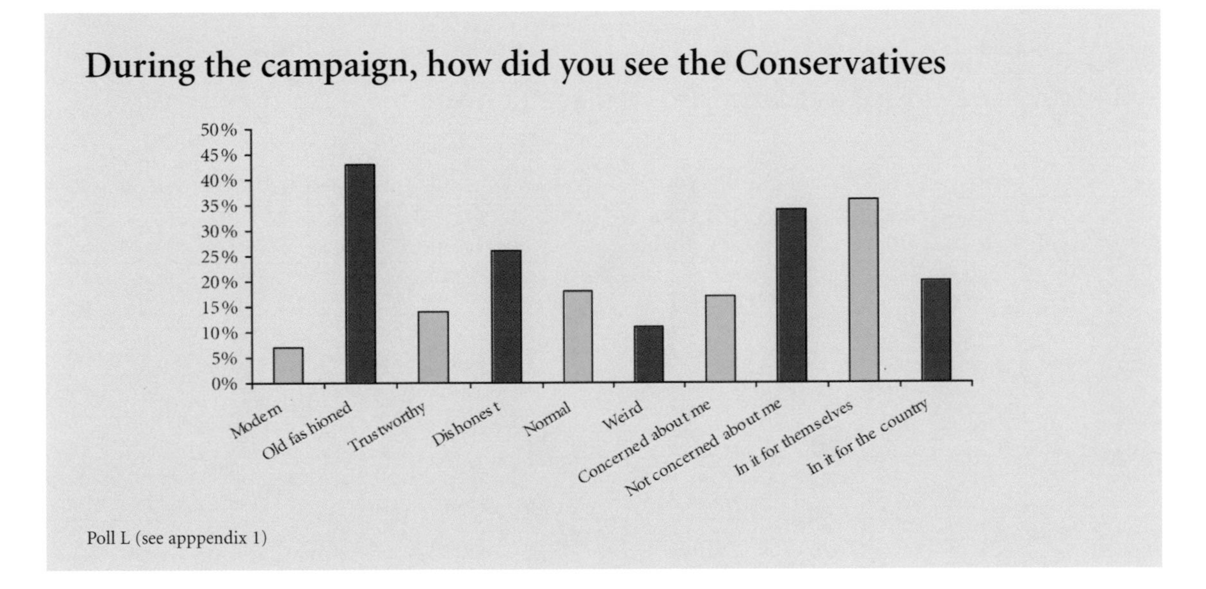

During the campaign, how did you see the Conservatives

Poll L (see apppendix 1)

Opinion in these battleground seats was evenly divided as to whether the Labour campaign was positive or negative (24% each), but it was clearly seen as both more positive and less negative than the Conservatives'. The same was true of the proportions who had seen the Labour campaign as aggressive and moderate (20% each). Similar numbers considered the campaign clear (16%) and confused (29%) as had been the case for the Conservatives, and while the same proportion thought it sloppy, more (though only 20%) had considered it professional. The same dismal proportion found Labour's campaign uplifting as said the same of the Conservatives, but marginally fewer (25%) said they actually found it depressing.

More than a quarter (26%) thought that Labour had come across as modern during the campaign, compared to only 7% who saw the Conservatives in the same way, and only 4% had considered Labour old-fashioned – less than a tenth of the Conservative figure. However, they were less likely than the Conservatives to be thought trustworthy (11%) and more likely to be seen as dishonest (37%). No fewer than 25% of voters thought Labour seemed normal, with only 3% considering the party weird (less than a third of the level for the Conservatives). As with the Tories, twice as many people thought the Labour Party was not concerned about people like them (36%) as thought it was, and while the same proportion as for the Conservatives thought Labour were in it only for themselves (36%), a slightly higher proportion (25%) thought the party had the interests of the country at heart than thought the same of the Tories.

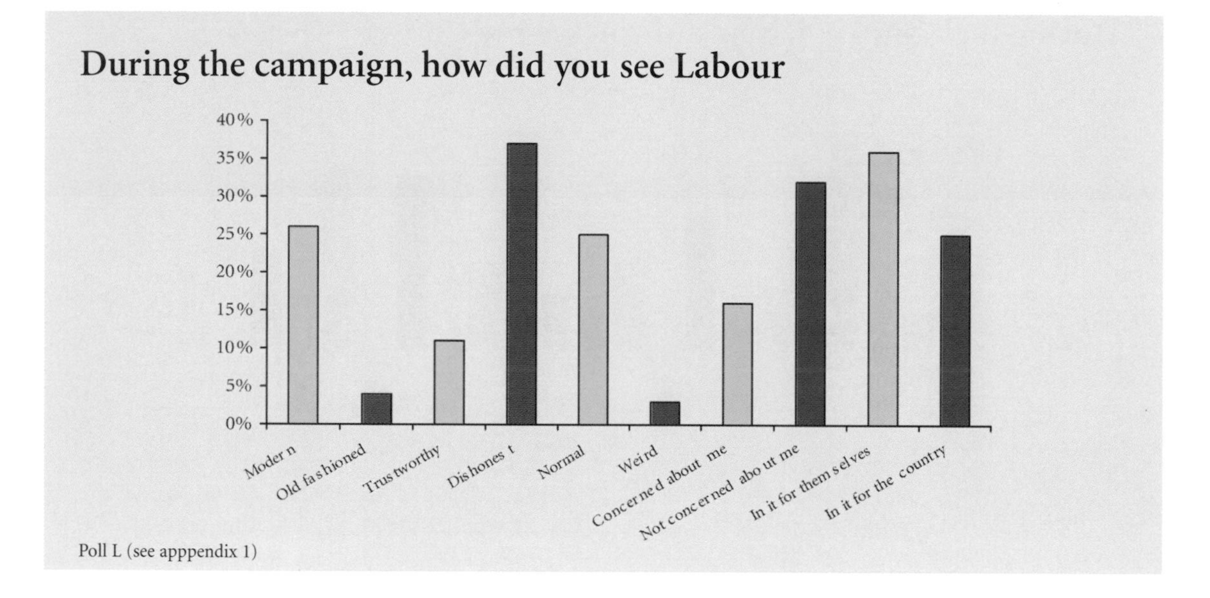

Poll L (see apppendix 1)

In stark contrast to their descriptions of Labour and the Conservatives, the most common adjectives people chose for the Liberal Democrat campaign in the Labour-Conservative battleground seats were "positive" (36%) and "moderate" (32%), dwarfing the proportions who considered it negative (8%) and aggressive (4%). It was also considered clearer (21%) and less confused (23%) than those of its bigger rivals. While only one in ten found the Liberal Democrat campaign depressing, the same proportion found it uplifting – more than double the number who said the same for Labour and the Conservatives.

The Liberal Democrats themselves came across in a correspondingly positive light. By considerable margins voters felt the Liberal Democrats appeared modern rather than old fashioned (29%-12%), trustworthy rather than dishonest (30%-5%), normal rather than weird (32%-9%), concerned rather than not concerned about people like them (29%-13%) and in it for what is best for the country rather than for themselves (34%-11%).

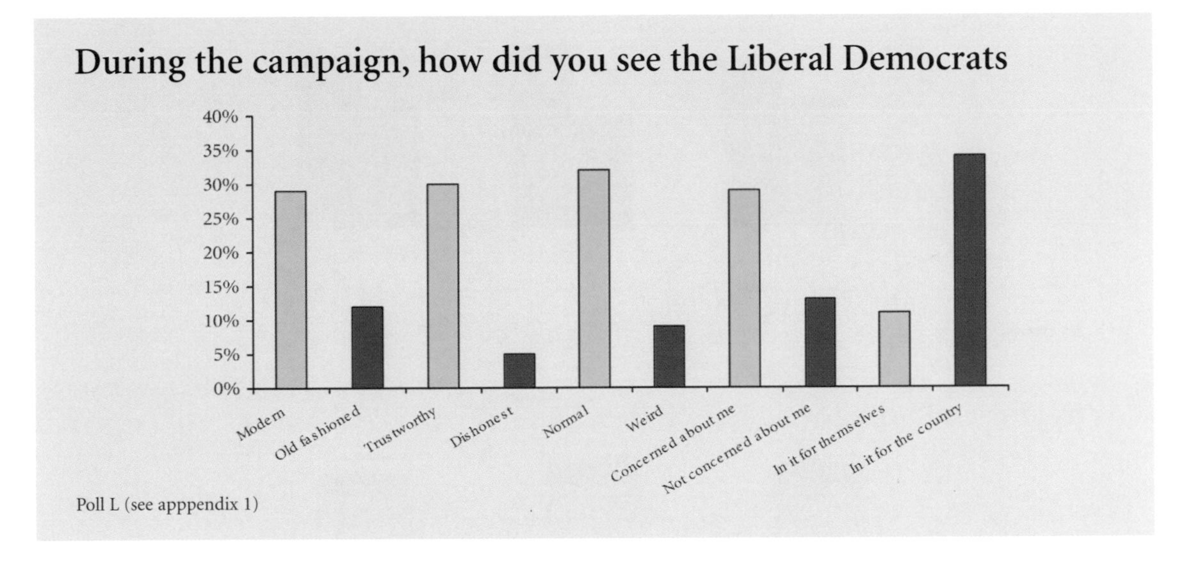

Poll L (see apppendix 1)

Come On You Reds

A clear majority of voters in the 130 Labour-Conservative battleground constituencies wanted Labour to win the election, especially voters aged 18-34, who preferred Labour to the Conservatives by 65% to 35%, and those in social groups C2DE (64%-36%). Liberal Democrat voters wanted a Labour rather than a Conservative government by 72% to 28%. Even in the top 40 Conservative targets, voters preferred a Labour government by 56% to 44%.

More than half of those who voted Labour or Conservative did so because they felt confident the party "would do a good job of running the country", with around another third in each case saying they were not confident the party would do a good job but that "they were better than the alternatives".

More than half of Liberal Democrat voters backed the party for reasons other than that they were confident the party would do a good job of running the country. 42% said that though they were not confident in the Liberal Democrats they were better than the alternative. In each case up to one in ten voters actually felt negative about the party they voted for, but disliked the others even more.

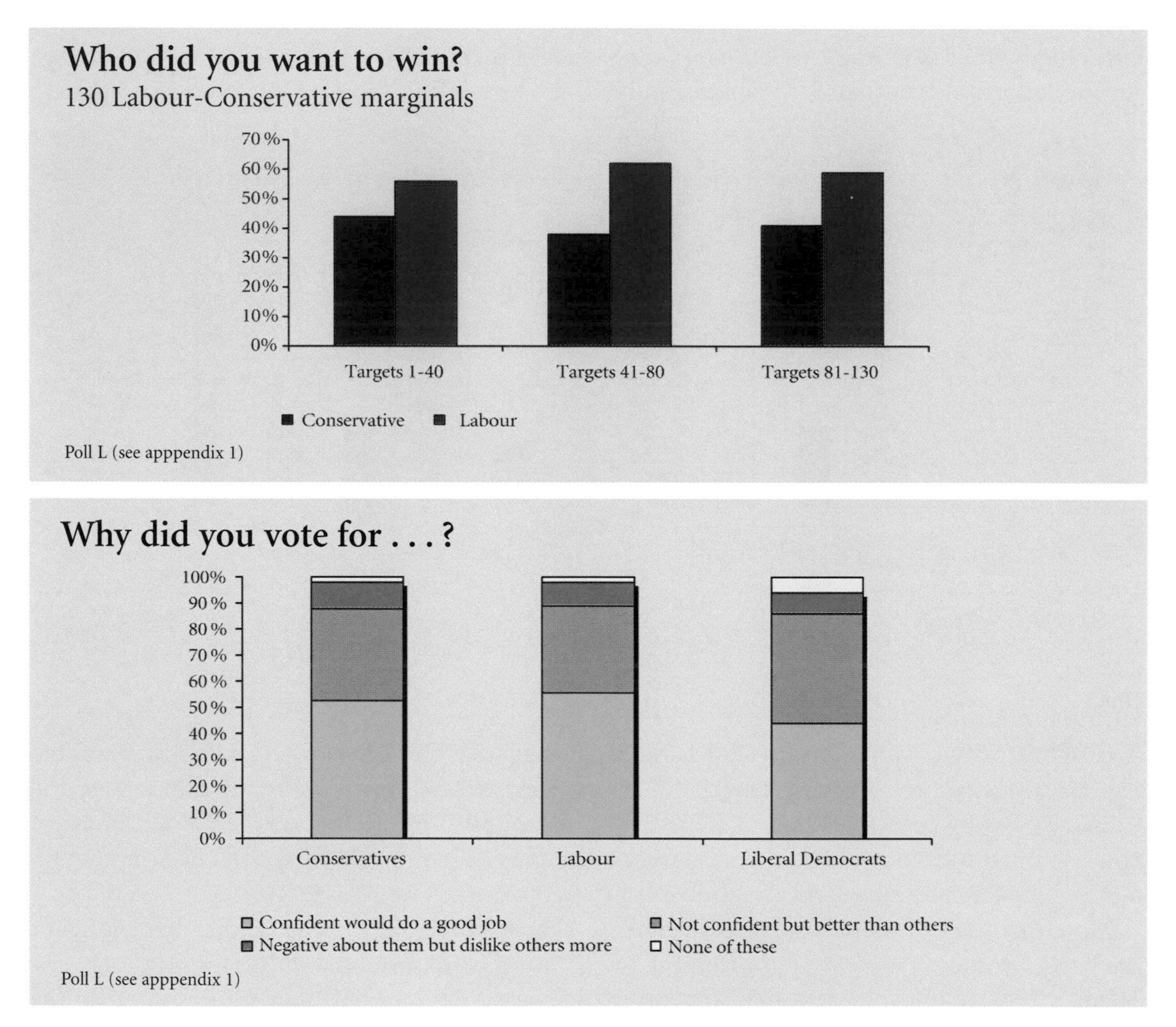

The Issues That Mattered

The post-election battleground survey also provided some telling data on what had motivated the supporters of each party. When asked "which one issue mattered most to you when deciding who to vote for?", 14% of all voters in these seats chose "pensions/social security/the minimum wage/poverty in Britain". Only 8% of Conservatives did the same, around half the proportion of Labour (17%) and Liberal Democrat (15%) voters who did so.

A fifth of Labour voters in these seats said "health/the NHS/hospitals" had been the most important issue to them, well above the overall level (12%) and well over double that among Conservative (7%) and Liberal Democrat (9%) voters.

Conservatives were disproportionately interested in immigration, with nearly a quarter (23%) saying it had been the issue that mattered most when deciding how to vote. This was nearly double the level for voters as a whole (12%) and nearly five times that of Labour and Liberal Democrat voters (5% each).

"Crime/law and order/police" was also more important to Conservatives than supporters of other parties, with more than twice as many Tories (15%) naming it as the issue that mattered most compared to 7% each among Labour and Liberal Democrat voters.

The same was true of "income tax/VAT/National Insurance/Council Tax", which was the most important issue to 18% of Conservatives, six times the level among Labour supporters.

Labour supporters were much more likely to have been interested in "economic growth/jobs/unemployment", with 16% saying it was the issue that mattered most to them, four times the level among Conservatives.

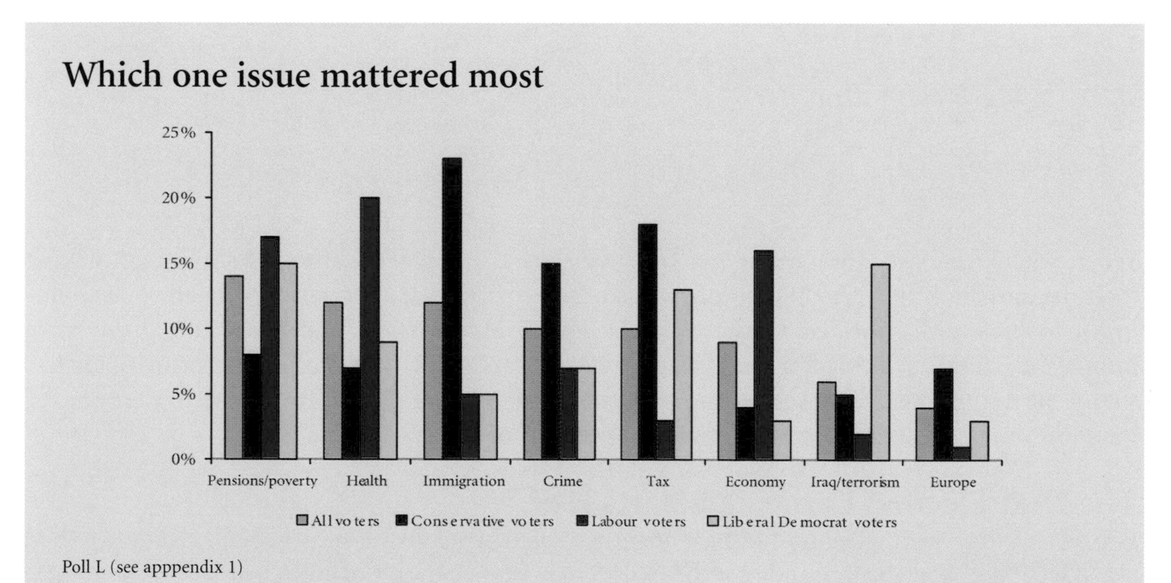

Which one issue mattered most

Poll L (see apppendix 1)

Liberal Democrat voters were particularly exercised by "Iraq/the war on terrorism". At 15%, the proportion of Liberal Democrats saying the issue was the most important to them was more than seven times as high as among Labour supporters (2%) and well over twice that among voters as a whole (6%).

"Europe/the EU constitution/the euro" had relatively little impact on most people's voting decisions, although for 7% of Conservatives it was the single most important issue.

Single most important issues, plus others that mattered a lot

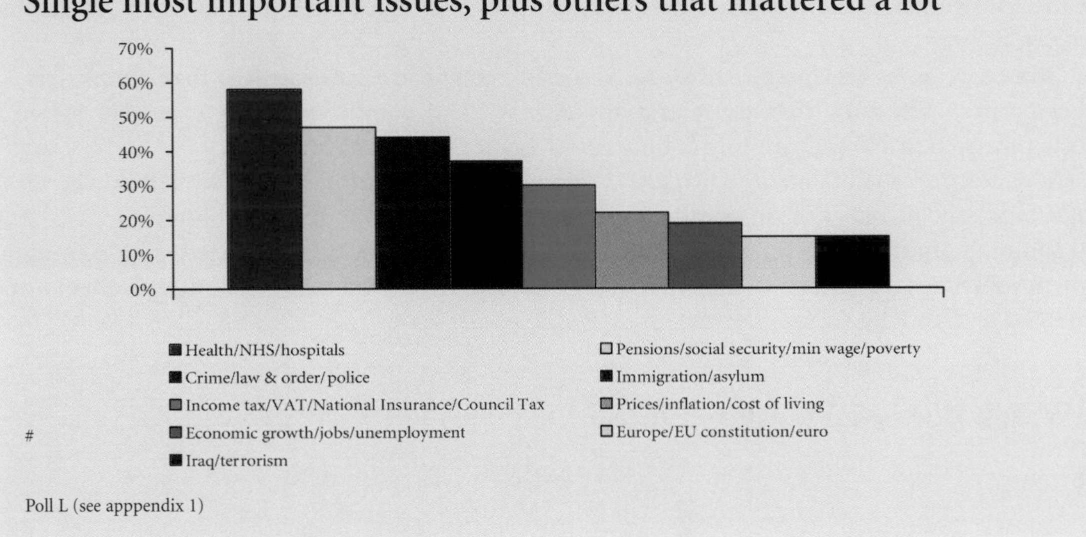

Poll L (see apppendix 1)

When voters were asked to choose two or three extra issues that "mattered a lot" when making their decision, health overtook pensions and social security, with a total of 58% of all voters naming it in their top priorities. Crime overtook immigration, which had been among the most important issues for 37% of voters (but 58% of Conservatives). Tax was a high priority for less than a third (but 44% of Conservative supporters), and Iraq and the war on terrorism were among the most important issues for 15% of voters (but 29% of Liberal Democrats).

The Next Election Campaign Starts Here

Few voters were willing to say for sure how they might vote at the next general election. When asked whether, "bearing in mind that the parties may change their policies, their leaders, and their general image", voting for each party would be certain, likely, possible, unlikely or completely ruled out, less than a fifth of voters would commit themselves. 9% said they were certain to vote Labour, 8% Conservative (including 13% of voters aged 55 and over) and 2% Liberal Democrat.

Labour were also ahead on likely voters, but not by much: adding those who were likely to those who were certain, Labour led by 27% to 23%, with the Liberal Democrats on 15%.

However, more than an additional third of the electorate (36%) said it was possible that they might vote for the Liberal Democrats next time – a higher proportion than for the Conservatives (21%) and Labour (27%). Similarly only 19% had completely ruled out the Liberal Democrats, while 21% had already decided against Labour and 27% against the Conservatives.

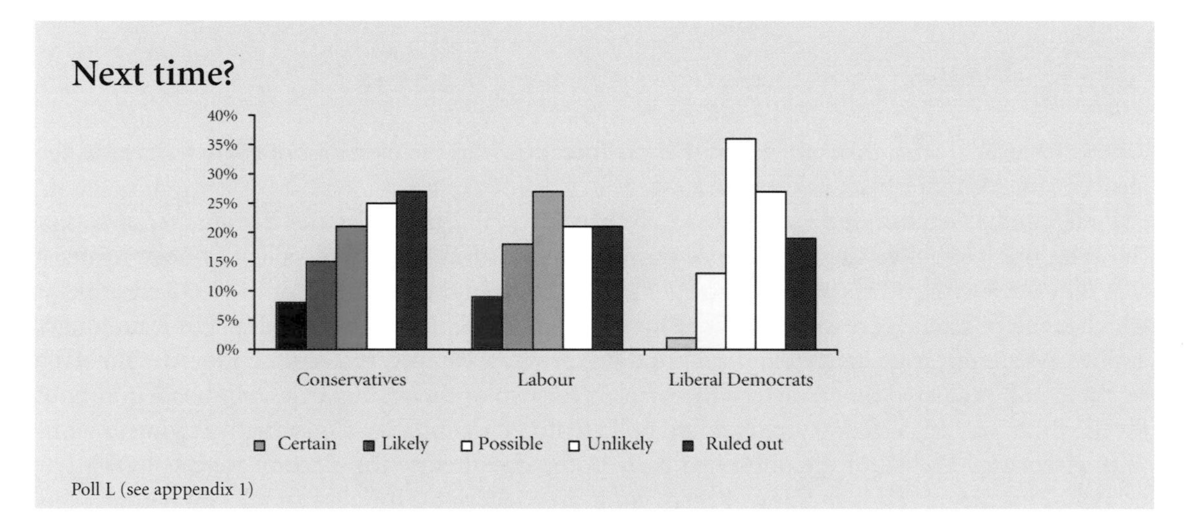

Poll L (see apppendix 1)

Adding together the "certain", "likely" and "possible" voters gives a picture of the potential support for each party at the next election. Using this method 54% of voters are potential Labour supporters, 51% potential Liberal Democrats and only 44% potential Conservatives. In other words, if everybody in Britain who currently thinks it is even possible that they might consider voting Conservative at the election actually does so, the party will get a similar share of the vote in 2008 or 2009 as it achieved in 1992.

It is on that note that I conclude this study. The Conservative Party must find a way to turn these potential supporters into real supporters. As important, it must reach people for whom voting Conservative is currently inconceivable.

I am encouraged that prominent Conservatives, including those contemplating standing for the leadership, have acknowledged these imperatives and are willing to discuss ideas as to how they

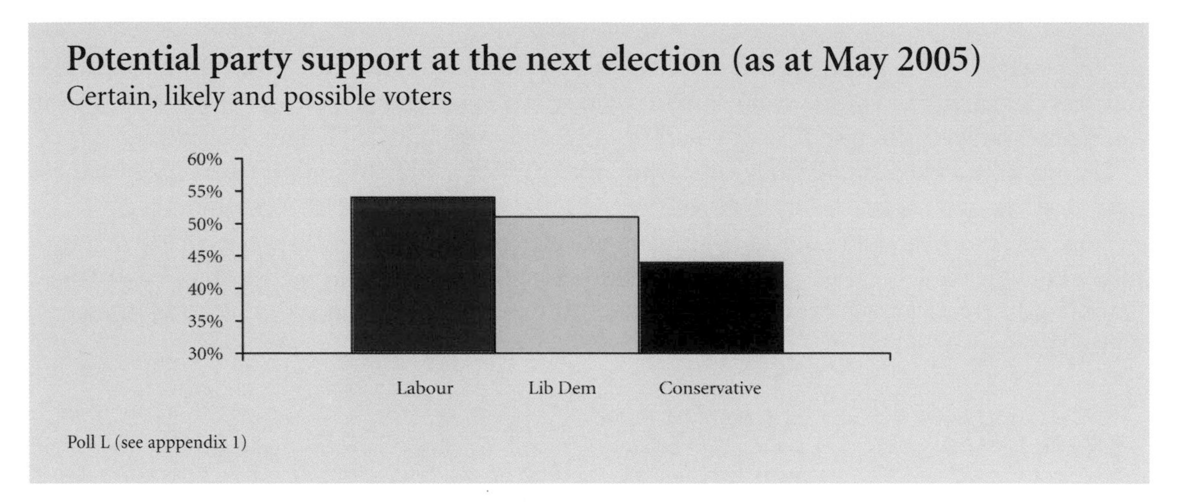

can be achieved. I wish them all well in their deliberations, and while I do not claim to have all the answers, in closing I offer two thoughts.

First, conducting opinion research and absorbing the findings does not denote credulity. For too long the instinctive Conservative response to unfavourable opinion polls has been to insist that they were wrong. This was a natural enough reaction in the aftermath of the 1992 election, at which some pollsters were so far out as to have predicted a Kinnock premiership, but it no longer applies. Methods have changed and poll findings are now often very accurate indeed. Our daily tracking poll predicted the result exactly correctly for two of the main parties and was 1 point out for the third; our pre-election battleground poll identified the Labour-Conservative swing to within one-tenth of 1%; all of the published polls in the days before the election were within a few points of the actual result and one of them got it precisely right. If polls can tell you within a few percentage points how millions of people are going to vote in a multi-party election, is it not possible that they are worth listening to?

Nor does opinion research represent for political parties some unspeakable betrayal of principle. Of course the duty of leaders is to lead, of course parroting phrases from focus groups is not a substitute for coherent policy, and of course politicians should be prepared to take a stand, argue for their convictions and change minds. But the idea that a party that finds out in a systematic and professional way what people are thinking has necessarily abandoned all belief is simply mad. For example, if during the last campaign common sense didn't tell the Tories that immigration was not bringing in the votes they needed and that calling the prime minister a liar was going to be counterproductive, opinion research would have done so and it would have told them why.

Polls won't tell the Conservatives everything they need to know and focus groups won't give them answers to all the problems of politics, let alone government. But they can help ensure that the party is talking about and developing principled Conservative policies on the things that matter to people, rather than the things it hopes can be made to matter. The Conservative Party regularly needs to ask itself - to coin a phrase - "Are we thinking what they're thinking?"

Secondly and finally, the party must appreciate the gravity of its situation. It will be tempting in the coming parliament for Conservatives to take comfort in the difficulties that will inevitably befall the government, or to assume that a faltering economy will eventually propel them back into power. To do so would be a disaster. There is no iron law of politics under which people automatically gravitate to the Conservatives when they are fed up with Labour governments. If there ever was, it is redundant. Anyone who doubts this fact needs only to look at the results of the 2005 election, when the Liberal Democrats' share of the vote rose by 3.8%, more than seven times the increase in support for the Tories.

So, faced with a government that had disappointed them and a prime minister they did not trust, why did people not vote in vast numbers for the party and the leader apparently in the best position to replace them? Our research over the last seven months shows the way towards the answers, not the least of which was that the Conservatives did not talk about the things that mattered to people in a way that showed that they recognised either their anxieties or their aspirations. But it would be a mistake to imagine that the issue is just one of presentation. The problem was not that millions of people in Britain thought the Conservative Party wasn't like them and didn't understand them; the problem was that they were right.

Appendix 1: Research Commissioned for this Study

	Date	Sample	Universe	Conducted by
A	5-9 November 2004	2,304	130 Lab-Con marginals 34 Lib Dem-Con marginals	YouGov
B	29 October- 3 November 2004	1,501	130 Lab-Con marginals 34 Lib Dem-Con marginals	Populus
C	22 November- 4 December 2004	2,004	9 Con-Lib Dem marginals	Populus
D	12-20 January 2005	10,007	Great Britain	Populus
E	21-25 February 2005	3,725	130 Lab-Con marginals	YouGov
F	7 January-4 May 2005	250 per day	Great Britain	Populus
G	29 March-5 April 2005	3,445	130 Lab-Con marginals	YouGov
H	27-29 April 2005	3,027	130 Lab-Con marginals	You Gov
I	February-April 2005	18,000	12 Lab-Con marginals	Populus
J	February-April 2005	12 focus groups	Undecided voters in 6 Labour marginals	Populus
K	6-9 May 2005	2,042	Great Britain	Populus
L	10-14 May 2005	4,592	130 Lab-Con marginals	YouGov

Appendix 2: Note on Methodology

The Populus Polls

(B, C, D, I, J and K)

Telephone Polls

The Populus polls were conducted by telephone using random digit dialling. This means that random samples were drawn from the BT database of telephone numbers, and each number so selected had its last digit randomised in order to provide a sample including both listed and unlisted numbers.

Weighting Data

All data were weighted to the profile of all British adults aged 18+ (including non telephone-owning households) or, in the case of polls in individual constituencies, the adults in those constituencies. Data were also weighted by sex, age, social class, household tenure, work status, number of cars in the household and whether or not the respondent has taken a foreign holiday in the last 3 years. Targets for these nationally weighted data were derived from the National Readership Survey, a random probability survey comprising 34,000 face-to-face interviews conducted annually. Targets for individual constituency polls were drawn from data supplied by the Office for National Statistics.

Voting Intention

Data were further weighted to ensure that they were as politically representative as possible on the basis of past vote. Some people forget who they voted for so Populus does not weight to the actual result of the last election but uses a "base weight" but to a figure between recalled past vote and the actual result. This figure is derived from a range of voting surveys and analysis of large samples of aggregate data from various points between elections.

Populus derives voting intention from four questions. Respondents are asked whether they voted at the last election and for whom, who they would support in a new election and how likely it is that they will actually vote. Figures are calculated after excluding those who will not vote, refuse to answer the question or say they don't know who they would vote for. The figures are also adjusted for turnout on the basis of respondents' declared likelihood of voting.

In a further step intended to address the tendency for "spirals of silence" among supporters of unpopular parties causing an inadvertent bias in the figures, Populus takes those who say they that they are going to vote at the next election but refuse to say how, and reallocates them to the party they voted for at the previous election at a value of 0.6.

Daily Tracking Poll

The approach of polling 250 voters a day, rolled into a 4-day 1,000 sample poll is designed to follow the movements of the campaign as it unfolds while also minimising, though not eliminating, volatility arising from the small daily sample size. All tracking polls conducted on this basis carry the risk that, because of the small sample size and relatively large margin of error, unexpected swings can sometimes occur. However, over the course of several days the tracking corrects itself and over the course of campaign its narrative will be revealing and broadly accurate.

More information on the methodology used in Populus polls can be found at www.populus-limited.com

The YouGov Polls

(A, E, G, H and L)

Internet Polls

YouGov conducts opinion research via an online panel of more than 90,000 voters throughout Great Britain. Each poll is conducted among a sub-sample of this panel that is representative of the electorate in the areas polled (for this study, a selection of marginal seats across the country).

Weighting Data

Data is weighted to the profile of all adults (including people without internet access), and to age, sex, social class, region, past vote and readership of individual newspapers.

Targets for the weighted data are derived from the census, the National Readership Survey and, for past vote, YouGov estimates derived from a comparison of voting intention of 5,000 respondents at the time of the 2001 general election with the responses from the same panel to later questions asking them to recall their 2001 vote.

For more information on the methodology used in YouGov's polls go to www.yougov.co.uk